1st Workshop on Speech and Multimodal Interaction in Assistive Environments 2012

(SMIAE '12)

Jeju Island, Korea
12 July 2012

ISBN: 978-1-62276-596-6

Printed from e-media with permission by:

Curran Associates, Inc.
57 Morehouse Lane
Red Hook, NY 12571

Some format issues inherent in the e-media version may also appear in this print version.

Printed by Curran Associates, Inc. (2012)

For permission requests, please contact the Association for Computational Linguistics at the address below.

Association for Computational Linguistics
209 N. Eighth Street
Stroudsburg, Pennsylvania 18360

Phone: 1-570-476-8006
Fax: 1-570-476-0860

acl@aclweb.org

Additional copies of this publication are available from:

Curran Associates, Inc.
57 Morehouse Lane
Red Hook, NY 12571 USA
Phone: 845-758-0400
Fax: 845-758-2634
Email: curran@proceedings.com
Web: www.proceedings.com

Preface

In recent years considerable progress has been made in speech processing and interaction as well as in multimodality. However, the application field of Assistive Environments has only recently become a focus for the speech and multimodality research community.

This workshop focuses on issues, applications, and development tools in the field of Speech and Multimodal Interaction in Assistive Environments (SMIAE). It is concerned with all topics which fit within the purview of speech and multimodal communication in environments suitable for the elderly and people with age-related physical or cognitive disabilities. Assistive environments are an application area of the research field of Ambient Assisted Living (AAL).

This research field is supported through a European technology and innovation funding programme, which promotes intelligent assistant systems for a better, healthier, and safer life in the preferred living environments through the use of Information and Communication Technologies (ICT). Human-computer and human-robot interaction are key technological tools in the area of Assistive Environments, and as such the workshop particularly aims to draw together speech and multimodal work in these areas. Moreover, we are delighted to have both theoretical and applied computational work regarding multimodal interaction in assistive environments at this workshop, including research fields like robotics, virtual environments, sociable agents, gesture, games, and mobile computing.

Dimitra Anastasiou
Desislava Zhekova
Cui Jian
Robert Ross

May 2012

Organizers:

Dimitra Anastasiou, Univeristy of Bremen, Germany
Desislava Zhekova, Indiana University, USA
Cui Jian, Univeristy of Bremen, Germany
Robert Ross, Dublin Institute of Technology, Ireland

Program Committee:

Jan Alexandersson, DFKI Saarbrücken
John Bateman, University of Bremen
Heriberto Cuayahuitl, DFKI Saarbrücken
Alexandre Denis, Loria-CNRS
Nina Dethlefs, University of Bremen
Eleni Efthimiou, Institute for Language and Speech Processing (ILSP) / R.C. "Athena"
Evita Fotinea, Institute for Language and Speech Processing (ILSP) / R.C. "Athena"
Konstantina Garoufi, University of Potsdam
Kalliroi Georgila, University of Southern California
Stefan Goetze, Fraunhofer Institute for Digital Media Technology
Florian Kretzschmar, Telekom Innovation Labs / Technische Universität Berlin
Susan Kemper, University of Kansas
Brigitte Krenn, Austrian Research Institute for Artificial Intelligence
Oliver Lemon, Heriot-Watt University
Ilias Maglogiannis, University of Central Greece
Patrick Oliver, University of Newcastle
Brian Roark, Oregon Health & Science University
Ruben San Segundo Hernandez, Technical University of Madrid
Matthias Scheutz, Tufts University
Hui Shi, University of Bremen
Kristina Striegnitz, Union College
Thora Tenbrink, University of Bremen
Mariët Theune, University of Twente
Pat Tun, Brandeis University Memory & Cognition Lab
Maria Wolters, University of Edinburgh
Wolfgang Zagler, Vienna University of Technology

Invited Speaker:

Mikio Nakano, Honda Research Institute Japan

Table of Contents

Workshop Program

9:00–9:10	Welcome and Introduction
9:10–10:00	Keynote: Robots that can learn new words and their grounded meanings through dialogues. Mikio Nakano
10:00–10:30	*Multimodal Human-Machine Interaction for Service Robots in Home-Care Environments* Stefan Goetze, Sven Fischer, Niko Moritz, Jens-E. Appell and Frank Wallhoff
10:30–11:00	Coffee Break
11:00–11:30	*Integration of Multimodal Interaction as Assistance in Virtual Environments* Kiran Pala, Ram Naresh, Sachin Joshi and Suryakanth V Ganagshetty
11:30–12:00	*Toward a Virtual Assistant for Vulnerable Users: Designing Careful Interaction* Ramin Yaghoubzadeh and Stefan Kopp
12:00–12:30	*Speech and Gesture Interaction in an Ambient Assisted Living Lab* Dimitra Anastasiou, Cui Jian and Desislava Zhekova
12:30–14:00	Lunch Break
14:00–14:30	*Reduction of Non-stationary Noise for a Robotic Living Assistant using Sparse Non-negative Matrix Factorization* Benjamin Cauchi, Stefan Goetze and Simon Doclo
14:30–15:00	*Towards a Self-Learning Assistive Vocal Interface: Vocabulary and Grammar Learning* Janneke van de Loo, Jort F. Gemmeke, Guy De Pauw, Joris Driesen, Hugo Van hamme and Walter Daelemans
15:00–15:30	*A Bengali Speech Synthesizer on Android OS* Sankar Mukherjee and Shyamal Kumar Das Mandal
15:30–16:00	Coffee Break
16:00–17:30	Discussion and Conclusion

Multimodal Human-Machine Interaction for Service Robots in Home-Care Environments

Stefan Goetze[1], Sven Fischer[1], Niko Moritz[1], Jens-E. Appell[1], Frank Wallhoff[1,2]
[1]Fraunhofer Institute for Digital Media Technology (IDMT), Project group Hearing, Speech and Audio Technology (HSA), 26129 Oldenburg, Germany
[2]Jade University of Applied Sciences, 26129 Oldenburg, Germany
{s.goetze,sven.fischer,niko.moritz,jens.appell,frank.wallhoff}@idmt.fraunhofer.de

Abstract

This contribution focuses on multimodal interaction techniques for a mobile communication and assistance system on a robot platform. The system comprises of acoustic, visual and haptic input modalities. Feedback is given to the user by a graphical user interface and a speech synthesis system. By this, multimodal and natural communication with the robot system is possible.

1 Introduction

The amount of older people in modern societies constantly grows due to demographic changes (European Commision Staff, 2007; Statistical Federal Office of Germany, 2008). These people desire to stay in their own homes as long as possible, however suffer from first health problems, such as decreased physical strength, cognitive decline (Petersen, 2004), visual and hearing impairments (Rudberg et al., 1993; Uimonen et al., 1999; Goetze et al., 2010b). This poses great challenges to the care systems since care services require a high amount of temporal and personnel efforts. Furthermore, older people living alone may suffer from social isolation since family members, friends and acquaintances may live at distant places and frequent face-to-face communication may be hard to realize.

It is nowadays commonly accepted that support by means of technical systems in the care sector will be inevitable in the future to cope with these challenges (Alliance, 2009). Examples for such assistive devices are reminder systems (Boll et al., 2010), medical assistance and tele-healthcare systems (Lisetti et al., 2003), personal emergency response systems, accessible human-machine interaction (Rennies et al., 2011) or social robotics (Chew et al., 2010).

This contribution describes the human-machine interaction modalities for a social robot called ALIAS (*adaptable ambient living assistant*) that is depicted in Figure 1. ALIAS is a mobile robot platform to foster communication and social interaction between the user and his/her social network as well as between the user and the robot platform. The aim of ALIAS is to ensure the maintenance of existing contacts to prevent social isolation instead of making human-to-human communication obsolete. ALIAS is supposed to act as a companion that encourages its owner to cultivate relationships and contacts to the real world.

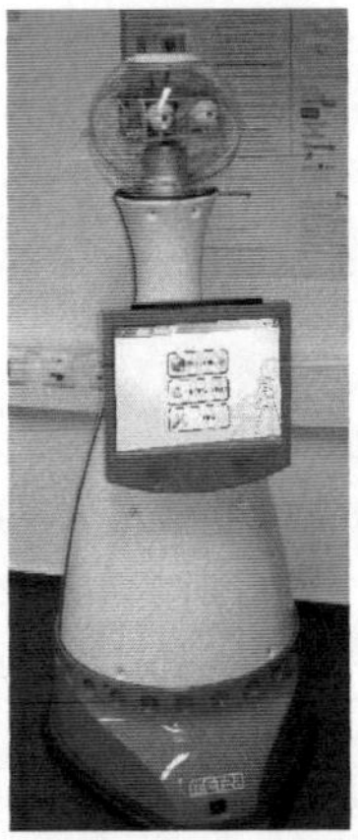

Figure 1: ALIAS robot platform.

Instead of classical interaction techniques solely

by using mouse and keybord, multi-modal human-machine interaction techniques allow for more natural and convenient human-machine interaction (Oviatt, 1999; Jaimes and Sebe, 2007; Goetze et al., 2010a). Especially for technology in the domain of ambient assisted living (AAL) which is mostly intended to be used by older users - these users often are less technophile than younger users (Meis et al., 2007) - multi-modal interaction strategies including modalities like speech and touch pads show high acceptance (Boll et al., 2010).

A touch display and a robust speech recognition and synthesis system enable the ALIAS robot platform to interact with the user via speech or using the mounted touch display (cf. Figure 1). Besides communication with the robot by speech input and output, communication with relatives and acquaintances via telephone channels, mobile phone channels and the internet is a central goal. An automatic reminder system motivating the user to participate actively in social interaction is developed. In addition, the user is encouraged to perform cognitive activities in order to preserve quality of life.

The following Section 2 briefly describes the system components of the ALIAS robot platform before Section 3 focuses on the multi-modal user-interaction strategies.

2 System Components and Applied Technologies

The ALIAS robot system has a variety of human-machine communication features and sensors. Figure 2 shows the general overview of the robots software modules which will be briefly introduced in the following.

The **dialogue manager** (DM) is the robot's most central component since it is the software module which is responsible for all decisions the robot has to take. Therefore, it is connected to almost every other module. The DM collects inputs and events from all these modules, interprets them, and decides which actions to perform, i.e. commands to send to which modules. It may move the robot to check on its user, initiate a video telephone call, or ask for a game of chess. The dialogue manager runs on the Windows computer, which is one of the two computer systems in the ALIAS system.

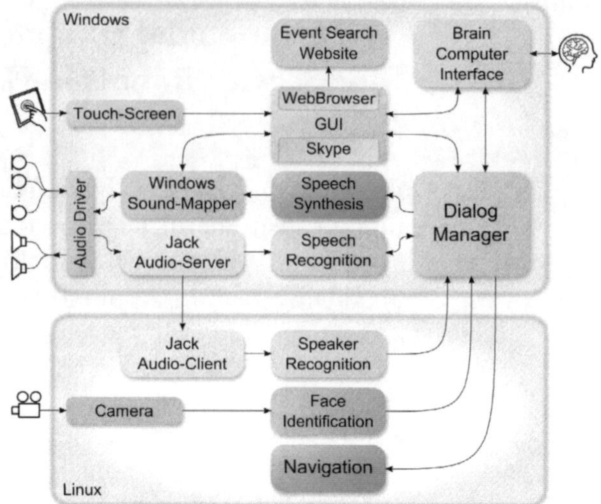

Figure 2: Overview of the ALIAS robot's software modules, distributed on two computers.

The **graphical user interface** (GUI) has a close link to the dialogue manager since it integrates several applications and receives user inputs of the Windows computer's operating system. Thus, it reacts to touch input and displays menus and all software modules with graphical output. (Section 3.1 provides more detailed information on the GUI.)

The **automatic speech recognition** (ASR) module enables the robot to understand and react on spoken commands (Moritz et al., 2011). It receives recorded audio signals from the Jack audio-server and converts it to a textual representation of spoken words. This list of recognized words will be sent to the DM for interpretation (cf. Section 3.2 for details).

The **speech synthesis** module enables the robot to communicate with its owner verbally (together with the ASR sytem). Speech synthesis (Taylor, 2009) is the artificial production of human voice. Text-to-speech (TTS) systems are used to convert written text into speech. An advanced system should be able to take any arbitrary text input and convert it into speech, whereby the language of the text must be known to be able to create the correct pronunciation. Several systems for speech synthesis are already commercially available to realize such a system. Speech output was found to be a desired user interaction strategy for assistive systems (Goetze et al., 2010a) if output phrases are properly designed since there's no need to reach out for the robot's display unit in order to interact with it.

A link to the world-wide web is established by integration of an easy-to-use **web browser** which is seamlessly integrated into the GUI. To counteract isolation an **event search web service** was realized (Khrouf and Troncy., 2011) that visualizes various events and corresponding pictures to the user that have taken place or will take place close to the user's location. To achieve this the robot connects to an online event search service. The service will provide him/her with a personalized selection of social event near his/her current location and personal preferences.

An input modality suitable for users that are unable to touch the robot's screen or to verbalize a speech command (e.g. after a stroke) is the **brain computer interface** (BCI) of the robot (Hintermüller et al., 2011). It uses a set of electrodes placed on the user's skull to measure electrical responses of the brain. These electrical potentials are evoked by means of visual stimuli, e.g. flashing images on a control display. By focusing on certain items on the BCI control display the user's brain activity can control the GUI of the robot. The BCI may also be used for writing text messages which can be sent using the integrated **Skype**™ chat functionality of the robot.

To distinguish between its owner and other persons, the robot uses an acoustic **speaker recognition** module. This provides ALIAS with additional information which can be used to differentiate between persons and interprete multiple speech inputs according to their individual context.

In order to achieve more human-like characteristics, the robot uses a **face identification** module. So it is able to adjust its eyes to face the person it's talking to. The face detection algorithm utilizes the robot's 360° panorama camera located on top of the robot's head, and thus covers the robots surroundings, completely.

The **navigation** module handles the actual movement, collision prevention, and odometry of the robot. It drives ALIAS by plotting waypoints on a pre-recorded map. Obstacles are detected using ultra-sonic sensors, the laser scanner, and the front camera. In case the robot's path is blocked, the navigation module will plot an alternative route in order to reach the designated target location, evading the obstacle (Kessler et al., 2011). The navigation module may also be remotely controlled by another person in order to check on the robot's owner in case an accident has been detected or the owner has requested for help.

3 Multimodal Interaction Strategies

The robot's user interface features different input modalities; speech commands, the BCI, or the touch screen (GUI). For speech input, the ASR module processes the recorded speech commands and translates them into multiple textual representations, which are then sent to the DM for interpretation.

BCI and GUI include a display unit to provide feedback to the user. Thus they require an additional pathway for receiving commands from the DM. In case of the BCI, available items on its control screen may be switched by the DM to reflect the current dialogue state, i.e. a selection of audio books if the audio book module has been accessed. For the GUI, which integrates several software applications into one single module, there is also the possibility of non-user related events, such as incoming phone calls from the integrated Skype module. The GUI has to relay these events to the DM for decision.

All user inputs and relevant system events are gathered by the DM. As the ALIAS system's central control unit, the DM keeps track of all active robot modules and relevant sensor data. It merges all provided inputs, puts them into context, interprets them, and decides which actions to perform. Whereas some inputs may be redundant, others may be invalid or highly dependent on the context.

For example, pushing a button on the touch screen is most likely related to the application that is running on the screen. Whereas the spoken phrase "on the right" could mean that the user wants ALIAS to push a button that is located on the right hand side of its screen. Another interpretation would be that the user wants the robot to turn to the right and move aside. Or the user was talking to another person in the room, possibly even on ALIAS' video telephone, and the spoken statement is not to concern the robot at all.

This section provides a closer look on the ALIAS robot's most frequently used user interfaces and their design.

3.1 Graphical User Interface

The GUI consists of a series of menus containing a few large buttons, each of them leading to another menu or starting an application, i.e. an integrated software module. The GUI's main menu is shown in Figure 3.

The GUI uses a minimalistic design, including some light gradients and blur for non-essential background components. Whereas the actual buttons feature comprehensive icons and text labels with large fonts, enclosed by high-contrast black frames. This eases distinction between buttons and background.

Taking visual impairments into account the GUI remains usable, while still being visually pleasing for people with unimpaired vision. Due to each users individual color perception, colors are used sparsely and mustn't be the sole cue to carry essential information. Instead combinations of colors, shapes, and labels are preferred.

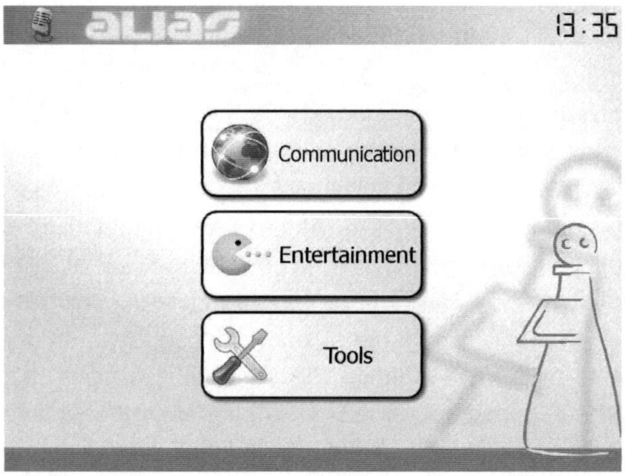

Figure 3: ALIAS robot's main menu.

The GUI depends on animations; buttons flash in a different (dark) colors when pressed and menus sliding on and off the screen when switched. Such animations provide visual feedback to user inputs and are unlikely to be missed by the user, since they involve the whole screen, usually.

The GUI makes a clear distinction between menus and application modules, though both are supposed to look quite similar on the screen. Menus provide access to sub-menus and integrated software modules i.e. applications, using a tree-like menu structure which is defined by a configuration file.

Application modules implement their very own individual layouts, buttons, features, and remote-control capabilities for the DM. By this, some features are available after the related application has been started, only. The GUI features a selection of integrated application modules, like a Skype™-based video telephone, a web-browser, a television module, an audio book player, a selection of serious games, and access to the robot's Wii gaming console.

The GUI processes two kinds of user inputs; direct inputs and indirect inputs. Both input types will be further outlined below.

3.1.1 Direct Inputs

The GUI accepts normal user inputs, as they are provided by the host computer's operating system. In case of the ALIAS robot the main source of such inputs will be the touch screen. These inputs are considered as direct inputs, since they are provided by the computer's operating system and are handled by the GUI directly.

More generally every input falls into the group of direct inputs if the GUI is directly receiving it. Accordingly even an incoming phone call is a direct input, because it is triggered by an integrated GUI module. So, unless properly handled and propagated, no other module would ever know about it. Thus, most direct inputs also need to be relayed to the dialogue manager that takes over the role of a state machine to keep all modules on the robot synchronized. If, for example, any input in the current situation is not allowed or even undesirable the DM can intervene and reject those inputs.

3.1.2 Indirect Inputs

A second kind of user inputs is represented by the group of indirect inputs. Indirect inputs are system messages, received by the GUI. Basically indirect inputs are inputs that are handled by another module, but require a reaction by the GUI. Typically such indirect inputs are generated by the Dialogue Manager, as response to a speech input for example.

The user may issue a verbal command to the robot: 'Call Britta, please!' The sound wave is picked up by the robot's microphones, converted into a sampled audio signal that is redirected by the Jack Audio Server to the speech recognition module. The speech recognition module converts the audio signal to a textual representation that will be interpreted and processed by the dialogue manager. In case the dialogue manager finds a contact named 'Britta' in its data base, it sends a series of network messages to the GUI, containing the required commands to bring up the telephone application and initiate the phone call.

3.1.3 Multi-modal Input

Most parts of the GUI can be controlled by touch display as well as by spoken commands. Furthermore, a control by the BCI is possible for parts of the GUI (currently Skype chat and entertainment such as audio books).

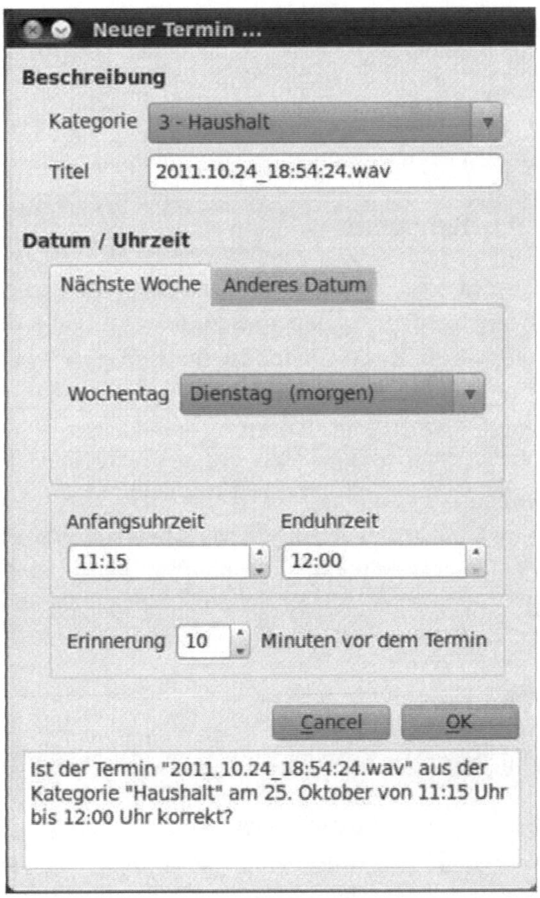

Figure 4: Multi-modal input dialog for appointments.

An example for a multi-modal interaction is the appointment input window depicted in Figure 4. It contains information about the category, the title, the start and end time of the appointment and a possibility to set a reminder. The interface can be controlled by mouse and keyboard as well as via speech commands following a structured dialogue. By this, the used is free to chose if he/she wants to use mouse and keyboard as a fast way to enter an appointment or speech if he/she is not close enough to the robot's touch display and is either not willing or not capable to reach it.

3.2 Speech Recognition

Creating an automatic speech recognition (ASR) device requires different processing steps. Figure 5 illustrates exemplary the structure of such a system.

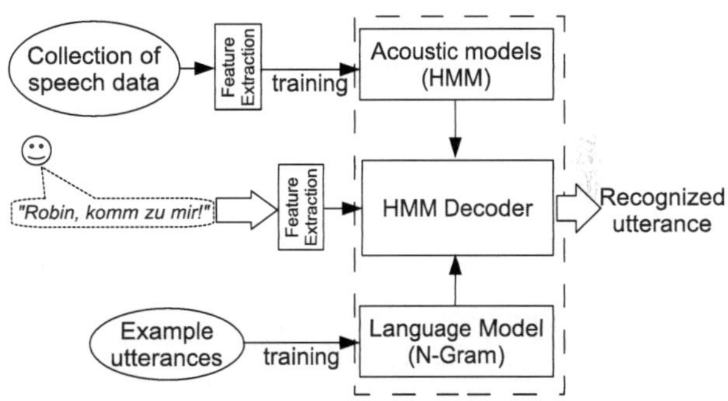

Figure 5: Schematic technical design of the ASR system.

A very important step is to collect a sufficiently large amount of speech data from many different speakers. This speech data is used to train the acoustic models, which in this case are hidden Markov models (HMM), and described in terms of well-known Mel frequency cepstral coefficients (MFCCs) (Benesty et al., 2008). Besides the HMM models of known words also so-called garbage models are trained, since the ASR device needs to be capable to distinguish not only between words that were trained from the training utterances but also between known and out-of-vocabulary (OOV) words.

In addition to the acoustic models a proper speech recognition system also needs a language model. The language model provides grammatical information about the utterances that are presented by the subjects to the ASR system. Language models can be separated into groups of statistical and non-statistical models. The ALIAS ASR system comprises of two recognition systems that are running at different grammatical rules (cf. Figure 6). The first ASR system uses a non-statistical language model that is typically used for ASR systems with small vocabulary size and very strict input expectations. This ASR system can be considered as a keyword spotter. In contrast, N-gram models can also be used for continuous speech recognition systems, where the grammatical information can get a lot more complex. Thus, the second recognizer uses statistical grammar rules (N-gram) which consists of a 2-gram forward and 3-gram backward model and enables the system to make a more soft decision on the recognized sentence.

By this two-way approach, the keyword spotting system can do a reliable search for important catchwords, whereby the second recognizer tries to understand more context from the spoken sentence. This ensures an even broader heuristic processing for the DM.

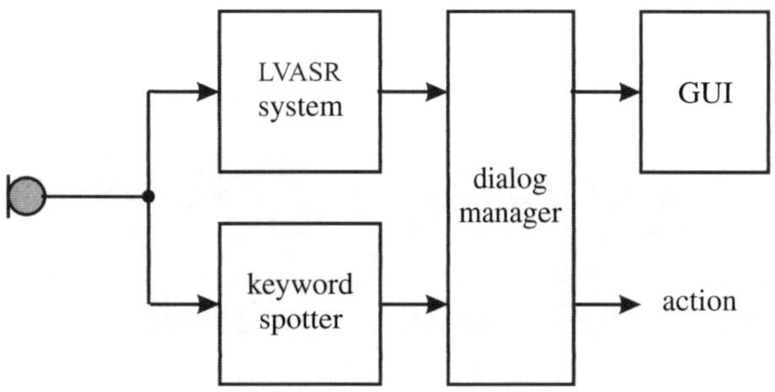

Figure 6: Two-way ASR system.

With the acoustic models and a valid language model the speech recognition device is now able to operate. The user utters any command, which is picked up by a microphone. Since in real-world scenarios the microphones do not only pick up the desired speech content but also disturbances like ambient noise or sounds produced by the (moving) robot system itself, the microphone signal has to be enhanced by appropriate signal processing schemes (Hänsler and Schmidt, 2004; Goetze et al., 2010a; Cauchi et al., 2012) before ASR features (MFCCs) are extracted from the speech input.A The extracted features are then transferred to the decoding system where the content of speech is analyzed.

ASR processing deals in terms of probabilities. Although speech recognition has been identified as a highly desired input modality for assistive systems (Goetze et al., 2010a) the acceptance drastically decreases if the recognition rate is not sufficiently high. For every acoustic input there are multiple recognition alternatives, with varying probabilities. Instead of using only the most probable recognition for output, the ASR module provides the DM with a few additional alternatives. This allows the DM a more thorough analysis and thus a more precise interpretation of the provided speech input to decide for an output on the GUI or an action (e.g. moving the roboter).

4 Conclusion

This paper presented multimodal interaction strategies for an robot assistant which has its main focus on support of communication. This includes both, fostering of human-to-human communication by providing communication capabilities over different channels and reminding on neglected relationships as well as communication between the technical system and its user by means of speech recognition and speech output.

Acknowledgments

This work was partially supported by the project AAL-2009-2-049 "Adaptable Ambient Living Assistant" (ALIAS) co-funded by the European Commission and the Federal Ministry of Education and Research (BMBF) in the Ambient Assisted Living (AAL) program and the by the project Design of Environments for Ageing (GAL) funded by the Lower Saxony Ministry of Science and Culture through the Niederschsisches Vorab grant programme (grant ZN 2701).

References

The European Ambient Assisted Living Innovation Alliance. 2009. *Ambient Assisted Living Roadmap*. VDI/VDE-IT AALIANCE Office.

J. Benesty, M.M. Sondhi, and Y. Huang. 2008. *Springer handbook of speech recognition*. Springer, New York.

S. Boll, W. Heuten, E.M. Meyer, and M. , Meis. 2010. Development of a Multimodal Reminder System for Older Persons in their Residential Home. *Informatics for Health and Social Care, SI Ageing & Technology*, 35(4), December.

B. Cauchi, S. Goetze, and S. Doclo. 2012. Reduction of Non-stationary Noise for a Robotic Living Assistant using Sparse Non-negative Matrix Factorization. In *Proc. Speech and Multimodal Interaction in Assistive Environments (SMIAE 2012)*, Jeju Island, Republic of Korea, Jul.

Selene Chew, Willie Tay, Danielle Smit, and Christoph Bartneck. 2010. Do social robots walk or roll? In Shuzhi Ge, Haizhou Li, John-John Cabibihan, and Yeow Tan, editors, *Social Robotics*, volume 6414 of *Lecture Notes in Computer Science*, pages 355–361. Springer Berlin / Heidelberg.

European Commision Staff. 2007. Working Document. Europes Demografic Future: Facts and Figures. Technical report, Commission of the European Communities, May.

S. Goetze, N. Moritz, J.-E. Appell, M. Meis, C. Bartsch, and J. Bitzer. 2010a. Acoustic User Interfaces for Ambient Assisted Living Technologies. *Informatics for Health and Social Care, SI Ageing & Technology*, 35(4):161–179, December.

S. Goetze, F. Xiong, J. Rennies, T. Rohdenburg, and J.-E. Appell. 2010b. Hands-Free Telecommunication for Elderly Persons Suffering from Hearing Deficiencies. In *12th IEEE International Conference on E-Health Networking, Application and Services (Healthcom'10)*, Lyon, France, July.

S. Goetze, J. Schröder, S. Gerlach, D. Hollosi, J.-E. Appell, and F. Wallhoff. 2012. Acoustic Monitoring and Localization for Social Care. *Journal of Computing Science and Engineering (JCSE), SI on uHealthcare*, 6(1):40–50, March.

E. Hänsler and G. Schmidt. 2004. *Acoustic Echo and Noise Control: a Practical Approach*. Wiley, Hoboken.

C. Hintermüller, C. Guger, and G. Edlinger. 2011. Brain-computer interface: Generic control interface for social interaction applications.

A. Jaimes and N. Sebe. 2007. Multimodal human-computer interaction: A survey. *Comput. Vis. Image Underst.*, 108(1-2):116–134, October.

J. Kessler, A. Scheidig, and H.-M. Gross. 2011. Approaching a person in a socially acceptable manner using expanding random trees. In *Proceedings of the 5th European Conference on Mobile Robots*, pages 95–100, Orebro, Sweden.

H. Khrouf and R. Troncy. 2011. Eventmedia: Visualizing events and associated media. In *Demo Session at the 10th International Semantic Web Conference (ISWC'2011)*, Bonn, Germany, Oct.

C. Lisetti, F. Nasoz, C. LeRouge, O. Ozyer, and K. Alvarez. 2003. Developing multimodal intelligent affective interfaces for tele-home health care. *International Journal of Human-Computer Studies*, 59(1-2):245 – 255. Applications of Affective Computing in Human-Computer Interaction.

M. Meis, J.-E. Appell, V. Hohmann, N v. Son, H. Frowein, A.M. Öster, and A. Hein. 2007. Telemonitoring and Assistant System for People with Hearing Deficiencies: First Results from a User Requirement Study. In *Proceedings of European Conference on eHealth (ECEH)*, pages 163–175.

N. Moritz, S. Goetze, and J.-E. Appell. 2011. Ambient Voice Control for a Personal Activity and Household Assistant. In R. Wichert and B. Eberhardt, editors, *Ambient Assisted Living - Advanced Technologies and Societal Change, Springer Lecture Notes in Computer Science (LNCS)*, number 978-3-642-18166-5, pages 63–74. Springer Science, January.

S.T. Oviatt. 1999. Ten myths of multimodal interaction. *Communications of the ACM. ACM New York, USA*, 42(11):74–81, Nov.

R.C. Petersen. 2004. Mild Cognitive Impairment as a Diagnostic Entity. *Journal of Internal Medicine*, 256:183–194.

J. Rennies, S. Goetze, and J.-E. Appell. 2011. Considering Hearing Deficiencies in Human-Computer Interaction. In M. Ziefle and C.Röcker, editors, *Human-Centered Design of E-Health Technologies: Concepts, Methods and Applications*, chapter 8, pages 180–207. IGI Global. In press.

M.A. Rudberg, S.E. Furner, J.E. Dunn, and C.K. Cassel. 1993. The Relationship of Visual and Hearing Impairments to Disability: An Analysis Using the Longitudinal Study of Aging. *Journal of Gerontology*, 48(6):M261–M265.

Statistical Federal Office of Germany. 2008. Demographic Changes in Germany: Impacts on Hospital Treatments and People in Need of Care (In German language: Demografischer Wandel in Deutschland - Heft 2 - Auswirkungen auf Krankenhausbehandlungen und Pflegebedürftige im Bund und in den Ländern). Technical report.

P. Taylor. 2009. *Text-to-Speech Synthesis*. Cambridge University Press.

S. Uimonen, Huttunen K., K. Jounio-Ervasti, and M. Sorri. 1999. Do We Know the Real Need for Hearing Rehabilitation at the Population Level? Hearing Impairments in the 5- to 75-Year Old Cross-Sectional Finnish Population. *British J. Audiology*, 33:53–59.

Integration of Multimodal Interaction as Assistance in Virtual Environments

[+]Kiran Pala
[+]Sachin Joshi
Ramnaresh Pothukuchi
[+]Suryakanth V Ganagashetty
[+]International Institute of Information Technology Hyderabad, Hyderabad India
{kiranap, rushtosachin, prnaresh.prnaresh} @ gmail.com, svg@iiit.ac.in

Abstract

This paper discusses the significance of the multimodal interaction in virtual environments (VE) and the criticalities involved in integration and coordination between modes during interaction. Also, we present an architecture and design of the integration mechanism with respect to information access in second language learning. In this connection, we have conducted an experiential study on speech inputs to understand how far users' experience of information can be considered to be supportive to this architecture.

1 Introduction

In the era of globalization education has taken a different path from the traditional space of teaching and learning. A nation's commerce and its market with respect to global changes, the implications of global needs are all demanding to policy makers for them to change educational policies accordingly.

In the above scenario, technology also has a significant role to play. Rapid development and use of new technologies have helped the human learning trajectory to take a complete shift from the classrooms to communities, personalization etc. There the e-learning and learning through technologies can be television and internet technologies, gadgets, tablets etc. E-learning has, with certainty, become a major entity in personal and community based learning. In addition, these days most of the classrooms have adapted itself to the concept of personalization with the help of technology assistive mechanisms in education, that is, the education sector shapes their face as e-education. Learning is a differently nuanced concept from teaching and instruction. Also, learning is a continuous interactive process; it cannot be a discretely developing process as we see that the definition of learning has shifted to a kind of entertainment activity. As shown in Pala (2012a) the interaction can be active or passive. We know that environments play a more significant role in facilitating the interaction with the learner as an interface between learners and communities. A learner receives information from environment through their senses such as visual, tactile and auditory with different activities which can directly affect their memory both declarative and procedural (Ullman, 2001). The activities blend with an interaction continuous with the environment. The tremendous development of information and communication technologies (ICTs) and its applications have made it possible to replicate the real environments on virtual platforms. The virtual environments facilitate the interaction for communication and information processing more or less like real environments.

Generally, whatever information is received through senses from the environment will be redirected to memory in the form of experience and then it is modulated with respect to the form of both production and perception states of a learner (Miller, and Johnson, 1976). But, whether the virtual environments provide an experience to the learners similar in these respects to the real environments is an answerable question to the community. Such experience is only possible when the multimodal interaction and assistance take place at the learner level from the environment. This communication, interaction and assistance can be peer-to-peer or person-to-person or peer-to-person etc. In any interaction or communication, assistance will be harnessed to rethink and rehearse the information which has been received. Since the rehearsal process is directly related to memory, it helps learner to be fluent and expert in the related domain.

2 Assistance in Accessing of Information

The assistive technologies played an important role in the olden days and even today with emerging information technology it does play a significant role. The assistive technologies are used not just for those who have physical or cognitive difficulties, but even in areas of information access and representation. Some of the assistive technological devices include speech recognition, screen reader, touch screen, on-screen keyboard, word prediction, transliteration etc. In the virtual environment, the resources considered are image database, text database, and video or action data (Bartle, 2004). VE will support the learner in many aspects and would boost learners' abilities. VE would be helpful in many ways such as providing immediate feedback, experimentation, grabbing focus, furthering exploration, and would also suit the learner requirements.

Accessing information and assistance with an eye on the representation of the accessed information is highly interrelated in "*understanding the meaning*". For example consider a sound-meaning relationship, if a naïve learner wants to learn the sounds of a new language and listens to a sound like */a/*. Users may not be able to immediately utter the same sound. For that we will use "*/a/* for */apple/*". Sometimes we need to show the picture of */apple/* also to make the learner better "*understand the meaning*" i.e. pragmatic information of the condition or statement like shown in figure-1. This instance easily and naturally occurs in real environments. But it is possible in VE by integrating multimodal interaction (tactile, visual, auditory) as assistance for the purpose of representing the accessed content from the crawled database extracted from the web according to the level of the learner and requirements like games or only content or meaning etc.

However, in the personalization of learning and facilitation according to content representations, the expected naturalness is still far away from what occurs in real situations. In this paper, we propose a naïve architecture with the reference to Indian languages and the target group is second language learners (L2).

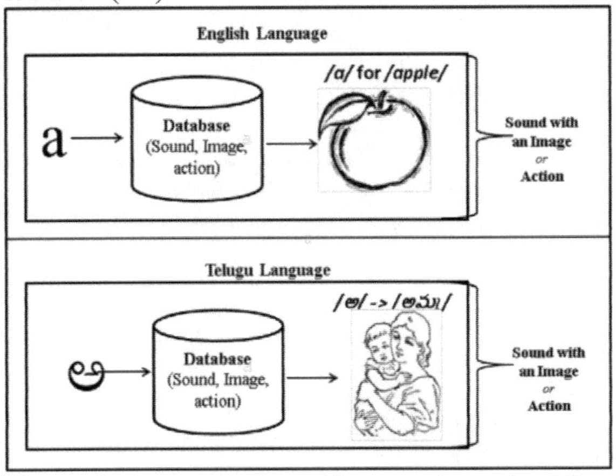

Figure 1: An example, environment required for understanding of the meaning with assistance.

3 Architecture

Here we discuss the details of the proposed architecture with the reference to each module's functions. This architecture mainly focuses on the integration of multimodal interaction as assistance to individuals who are adult learners. We have considered in the designing of this architecture learners' behavioral profiles, cognitive abilities and technological traits to pave the way for a more personalized interaction with the environment. Pala (2012a) has shown that these learners can be from any age group after the stage of puberty including even those who do not have much experience in use of virtual environments.

Input Devices: All these input devices like Automatic Speech Recognition (ASR) touch screen, mouse, keyboard etc. are interconnected to each other to ensure avoidance of information loss during non-linear interaction as well. Generally, adult individual learners move towards multitasking and non-linear interaction at a time and it has been expected that it should be a continuous activity. For example, the learner can give a speech input which is recognized by the ASR, at the same time the learner can utilize touch screen, keyboard and mouse to give another input. The input of the learner can be an alphabet or a word. Here we are dealing with sound-meaning relationships and conceptual structures and their types in languages at the lexical level. The multiple input facilities will assist the learner to provide versatile inputs of their own choice. It also has a significant role in furthering or initializing learning in learners who have physical disorders. This combined interaction of the visual and tactile senses is directly connected to the procedural memory (Christiansen and Chater, 2008; Tomasello, 2008).

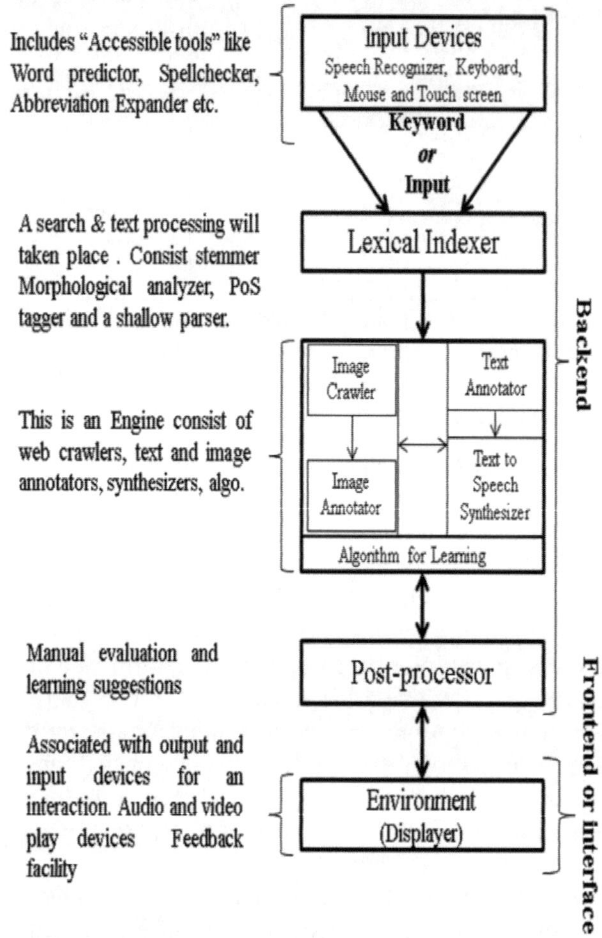

Figure 2: A Block diagram of Virtual Environment with Multimodal interaction as assistive.

Lexical Indexer: It is a kind of database with the linguistic categories and relations of each lexeme as has been discussed in Pala (2012b). It consists of a morphological analyzer and a stemmer. At the functional level it extracts the root word from the given input and verifies it in the indexer for its category and relationships in order to search for the same category-oriented examples and images from the web through crawlers. Additionally, the same keywords will be indexed again for ranking purposes of a specific learner. If a keyword is not available with the indexer, it sends the keyword directly to the web with a new index and later learns the relations and categories with the help of parts-of-speech taggers (POS) and shallow parses (Parser/Hindi, 2012; Akshar, Chaitanya, and Sangal, 1995).

An Engine: This engine consists of web crawlers for content resources, annotators, synthesizers (Text-to-Speech) and a predictive learning algorithm which has been built on self-organizing maps. Speech synthesizers receive information from the text annotator. The examples are provided in the form of phones, lexical items and sentences, it converts them into a signal form to speak it aloud when the learner requests.

Here annotators have a significant responsibility in handling information. In the process of building image annotators, we have used regular expressions for replacing the names. In addition, we have used wavelet transforms to verify the quality i.e. pixel depth, colors hue etc. of the image. Some other parameters like size and weight of the image have also been taken into account. Similarly, according to Pala (2011a) the text annotators have been constructed with an eye on parameters like removal of punctuations and special symbols etc. through an inclusion of the heuristic mechanism for anaphora references. The projection of video for action-related lexical items has been dealt with in the post-processing section.

Post-Processor: In this module we will have a verification process at initial stages, i.e., in the developmental state of the application a manual check up will be carried out along with auto verification process by the content developers who will look into the pragmatic and semantic aspects of example sentences, action videos and images very carefully. In the case of videos, the post-processing stage is more important in that when the input keyword contains a verb, making the action through image or text understandable is highly difficult. Thus, we have chosen the video form for lexical items related to action and motion. This categorical information will be received from the lexical indexer. The video codecs, definition of the video or animations quality, the length of the video and the mixture of audio clarity are very important parameters in selection and building of such action oriented contents.

In this paper we are dealing with the content representation modes but there is a similar significant role that mediates having a "*kind of content and presentation model for presenting to understand the meaning*" in learning process. This will streamline the process of the constant review process by the domain experts as shown in Pala (2012b).

Displayer: It is a space to interact with the user or the leaner, i.e., it is an interface between the learner and the application. It is embedded with all interaction modes (input and output tools) which we have discussed above for the assistance purpose. It projects the output in all types of modes which affect different senses (visual and auditory) of the user on screen according to user input requests. The displayer is crucial as the learners get distracted and lose interest in learning if the size of the screen, projection and the level of pixel value are to be defined according to user requirements. This requires a meticulous design so that the users' attention and their rehearsal activity gravitate towards the learning content.

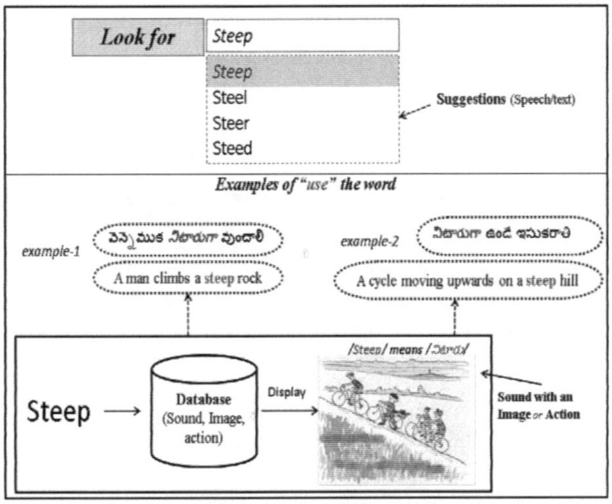

Figure 3: Example for Bilingual environment (English to Telugu)

Since this application is multilingual, the learner can make a request in any language. At this moment we have built an application for two major Indian languages and English. If, for example, a user asks for a meaning and use of the lexical item in English and their target language is Telugu, the "meaning" and "use" of the lexical items will be shown in what we see in figure-3 below. Native speakers generally look for the synonym for a "regular use" of a lexical item. We consider this factor to be of much importance and build a database which consists of the synonyms with their "regular use" as shown in the figure-4 below.

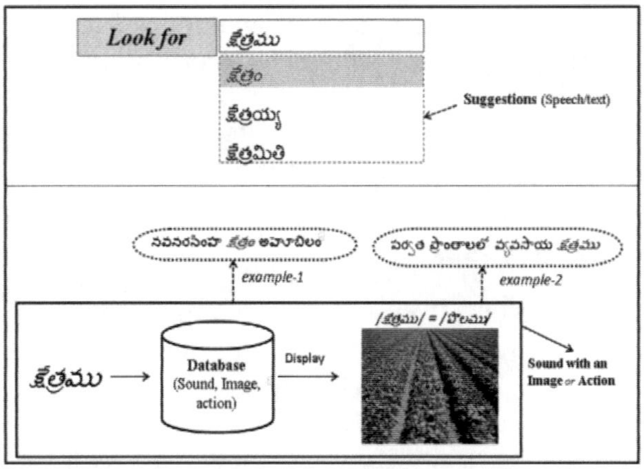

Figure 4: An example process of monolingual environment (Telugu to Telugu (Robert and Wyatt, 1956))

4 User Experience Study on Multimodal Interaction

To demonstrate the impact of multiple input modes on the quality of users' experience we have performed an experiential study to elicit users' perceptual inference- through speech and keyboard. We have built an English ASR using CMU Sphinx. For this we have used 1000 isolated words for the testing of the ASR which is used for training. The study was executed by providing the isolated words recorded by speakers. In this study we have passes since we would like to test user experience after the integration of the multimodal input mechanisms (here we have integrated a keyboard with ASR) to an individual computer. In the first pass the spoken word was decoded using the entire vocabulary of 1000 words given to the recognizer. Then the user was asked to type the first character of the spoken word. The words starting with that character were segregated. In second pass, the spoken word was decoded with only segregated words given as input vocabulary to ASR. As expected, the second pass decoding showed a major accuracy improvement because of reduction in search vocabulary size. The relative improvement in accuracy was 36.61% percent. The entire procedure has been designed in such a manner that each lexical item will be selected from a bag of lexical items. As the entire procedure is executed, significant parameters for evaluation of the responses from the participants are drawn up for further analysis. All users reported that they were much more satisfied with multimodal items than with using speech recognition alone, since the system performs better with a minimal additional effort of pressing a single key. Not only accuracy but speed of the system was better.

5 Implications

Results accrued from such a study are believed to have ramifications for the interface between decision making behavior at the level of the individual and the organization in a more specific sense. Thus this observation shows that multi-modal interfaces can lead to better user experience. Human experience is labile and malleable in that it can be harnessed in different modes and through different media with the added advantage that the same content can be harnessed, molded and manipulated for differentially oriented purposes and tasks at hand. This character of experience is fine-tuned for multimodal learning of linguistic structures the underlying cognitive structures of which can be observed to shape and be reshaped by such experiences in VEs as the study has revealed. This is extremely valuable for any study that aims at figuring out how cognitive structures during learning can be seen to behave in vivo.

6 Future Work

There are several limitations and problems with the current study. Language learning especially lexical learning is a very complicated and multi-dimensional process requiring representationality at several levels of architectural specification. This has been attenuated by orders of magnitude for the sake of modeling and initialization of the processes within the architecture of the current VE. This needs a further elaboration within the current architecture that will lead to multi-layered sub-architectures for lexical learning cutting across syntactic, morphological, semantics/pragmatic and other cognitive levels of representation.

References

Akshar, B, Chaitanya, V and Sangal, R., 1995, Natural Language Processing: A Paninian Perspective, Prentice-Hall of India, New Delhi, 65-106.

Bartle, R.A., 2004, Designing virtual worlds, New Riders Pub.

Christiansen, M.H. and Chater, N., 2008, Language as shaped by the brain. Behav. Brain Sci. 31, 489–509

Miller, G, Johnson, L. P., 1976., Language and Perception. Cambridge: Cambridge University Press.

Pala. K., and Gangashetty S.V., 2012a (In Press), Virtual Environments can Mediate Continuous Learning, Technology Inclusive Learning. IGI, USA.

Pala K., Gangashetty S.V., 2012b (In press), Challenges and Opportunities in Automatically Building Bilingual Lexicon from Web Corpus, in Interdisciplinary Journal on Linguistics, University Press.

Pala, K. and Begum, R., 2011a An Experiment on Resolving Pronominal Anaphora in Hindi: Using Heuristics, Journal on Information Systems for Indian Languages, 267-270, Springer.

Pala, K. and Singh, A.K. and Gangashetty, S.V., 2011b, Games for Academic Vocabulary Learning through a Virtual Environment, Asian Language Processing (IALP), 2011 International Conference on, 295-298, IEEE

Parser/Hindi, 2012, Hindi Shallow Parser source, Retrieved 1 March 2012 from, Hindi Shallow Parser-source, http://ltrc.iiit.ac.in/analyzer/

Robert, C. and Wyatt, JL, 1956, A Comparative Grammar of the Dravidian or South Indian Family of Languages, Robert, Revised and edited by Rev, JL Wyatt and T. Ramakrishna Pillai, Reprint ed., (Madras:. University of Madras, 1961)

Tomasello, M., 2008. The Origins of Human Communication, MIT Press

Ullman, M.T., 2001. The Declarative/Procedural Model of Lexicon and Grammar, Journal of Psycholinguistic Research, 30(1).

Toward a Virtual Assistant for Vulnerable Users: Designing Careful Interaction

Ramin Yaghoubzadeh
Sociable Agents Group, CITEC
Bielefeld University; PO Box 100131
33501 Bielefeld, Germany
ryaghoub@techfak.uni-bielefeld.de

Stefan Kopp
Sociable Agents Group, CITEC
Bielefeld University; PO Box 100131
33501 Bielefeld, Germany
skopp@techfak.uni-bielefeld.de

Abstract

The VASA project develops a multimodal assistive system mediated by a virtual agent that is intended to foster autonomy of communication and activity management in older people and people with disabilities. Assistive systems intended for these user groups have to take their individual vulnerabilities into account. A variety of psychic, emotional as well as behavioral conditions can manifest at the same time. Systems that fail to take them into account might not only fail at joint tasks, but also risk damage to their interlocutors. We identify important conditions and disorders and analyze their immediate consequences for the design of careful assistive systems.

1 Introduction

In 2001, the World Health Organization consolidated previous taxonomies of somatic and mental functions and the everyday needs of human beings into the comprehensive International Classification of Functioning, Disability and Health *ICF* (WHO, 2001). Older people, as well as people with impairments, often need support from others to satisfy those basic needs, among which are activities related to self-care, to mobility, but also to communication and management of the daily activities and the social environment. For many older people, a catastrophic event, most often either a fall or the passing of their spouse, leads to their sudden loss of autonomy and subsequent submission into stationary care. In the latter case, the loss of their day structure is frequently the intermediate cause. The same effect can be observed for many disabled people of all ages who must make a transition from assisted living to stationary care. Here, specialized systems that assist in preserving autonomy in a spectrum of daily need fulfillment can potentially be of great benefit.

The present paper introduces the VASA project ("Virtual Assistants and their Social Acceptability"), which in cooperation with a health-care foundation examines how both older patients and people with various impediments, congenital or acquired, both in stationary and assisted living, can be provided with technical assistance to maintain autonomy for as long as possible. Importantly, we are not focusing on physical assistance, but on supporting a person's capability for organizing a social environment (WHO ICF d9205: 'Socializing') and managing the day structure generally (d230: 'Carrying out daily routine'). These two tasks turned out to be crucial in our analysis with the health care personnel. We thus aim to develop an assistive system for (1) managing daily routine and weekly appointments with the user, and (2) accessing a video call interface for contacting acquaintances or care personnel (d360: 'Using communication devices and techniques').

But how should such a system meet its user, and what criteria should guide the system interface design? Research has shown that older users are far more likely to employ a 'social' conversation style with a system (Wolters et al., 2009). The VASA project explores the use of a "virtual assistant", an humanoid conversational agent that features natural-language and touchscreen input and human-like communicative behavior (speech, gesture; see Fig. 1 for the current running prototype).

Figure 1: The VASA system. Left side: natural-language calendar management; right side: video call interface.

In this paper we review work on related systems for older people and people with disabilities. We then argue that beside the general goal of maximizing usability for this specific user group, there is an enhanced *vulnerability* of these users that calls for special care in interaction design; we substantiate this view by an analysis of potential mental conditions of the prospective users along with discussions of what requirements arise from them.

2 Related work

Generally, assistive systems are driven by task reasoning systems as well as components for human-computer interaction, which can be specialized for older or disabled persons. Modern systems that attempt to provide a "natural" interaction are being developed and evaluated, including touch-screen and haptic interfaces and interfaces capable of understanding and generating natural language, all of them providing an immediacy between communicative intentions and their execution that makes them suitable especially for users without technical expertise, with reduced sensorimotor skills or reduced capability for learning new interaction paradigms, as is frequently the case with older or impaired persons.

The performance of such systems in terms of suitable operation in interaction, successful task completion, and user-reported satisfaction, has been subject to systematic evaluation under controlled conditions: The performance of speech recognition systems has been compared between base-line users and people with varying degrees of dysarthria (breathiness, dysfluencies, involuntary noises). Off-the-shelf speech recognition systems have higher failure rates with dysarthric speakers (Raghavendra et al., 2001). Mildly and moderately dysarthric speakers can attain a recognition accuracy of 80% in dictation systems, breath exercises and phonation training improve performance (Young and Mihailidis, 2010). Vipperla et al. (2009) compared speech recognition for younger and older users, reporting an 11% baseline increase in word error rates for the latter group, attributed to both acoustic and linguistic causes. The Stardust project succeeded in very high single-word recognition rates on small dictionaries in patients with severe dysarthria, enabling them to control their environment by voice (Hawley et al., 2007). Fager et al. (2010) implemented a multimodal prototype system that combined ASR with a word prediction model and a capability to enter an initial letter, leading to an accuracy of $> 80\%$; noting that other conditions, such as a reduced visual field or ataxia, had to be addressed with technical solutions for each individual. Jian et al. (2011) designed a system for direction giving for seniors, suggesting specific design guidelines addressing typical perceptive, motor, attentive and cognitive impairments of older users. The evaluation of their multimodal system (speech and touch/image) led to positive results with respect to effectivity, efficiency and user-reported satisfaction.

3 Careful Interaction with Vulnerable People: Analysis

The more autonomously assistive systems act, the higher the potential negative effects they can consequentially cause. This is especially true for robotic systems, since their extension into the physical world entails possible harmful effects if proper reasoning or safety precautions should be breached by unanticipated events. But even without physical manipulation, real damage can still be done. This might be due to misunderstandings, leading to wrong assumptions in the system, and hence to actions being performed on behalf, but actually to the detriment, of the user. It might, however, also be due to the wrong things being communicated, or communicated in an inappropriate manner, leading to unnecessary negative appraisal, discomfort, or triggering of a negative psychic condition in the user. While unlikely to cause damage in an interaction with the average healthy interactant, this issue is of the utmost importance for many potential user groups.

Frail or potentially unstable users are arguably among those who can derive the greatest benefits from easily accessible assistive systems, enabling them to perform tasks which they might else not, or no longer, perform, thus preserving their autonomy. However, they are at the same time affected by a multitude of possible cognitive, psychic and emotional conditions and behavioral anomalies that can occur simultaneously. Each of these conditions entails special constraints for interactive systems, either for the interaction channels, for the contents, or for both. Several factors have been accounted for in existing systems: Reduced perceptive faculty (vision, hearing), reduced motor abilities (ataxia), and attention and memory impairments, mitigated by best-practice rules (Jian et al., 2011). Attempts to account for users with mild dementia have been made, such as in the ISISEMD project. Avoiding a deep hierarchy of dialogue structures and providing extra information (repetition, paraphrase) rather than maximum parsimony are paramount in cases of impaired memory and abstraction faculty, whereas people with learning difficulties need a system that operates without extensive training (of the user).

For systems that strive to provide long-term support to a specific person, adaptation to that person is of vital importance – by employing user models that are adapted either manually or using learning algorithms. System behavior should be adapted both in the content provided as well as the form it is provided in, to enable a working relationship that is both effective and pleasant for the user (Yaghoubzadeh and Kopp, 2011). This alone however is insufficient; since the vulnerability of the actual clientele in VASA is considerable, each of the encountered mental conditions has to be analyzed and additional dialogue constraints be enforced before autonomous interactions can be permitted. There is a variety of such factors that have not yet been comprehensively addressed, but might cause critical damage to some interactants if not considered. The following section captures the most frequently encountered phenomena, which were identified in dialogue with care personnel:

- **Depression and Bipolar Disorder:** Roughly ten percent of the population suffer from depression at some point in their lives. Depression increases the risk for suicide ten- to twentyfold (Sadock et al., 2007). Bipolar disorder manifests in episodic effects, where sensations of racing thoughts and heightened activity (mania) and listlessness and social passivity (severe depression) alternate or occur simultaneously; depressive relapses in particular are points of vulnerability (Hill and Shepherd, 2009). There are successes in detecting depressive states from facial and voice cues at $> 80\%$ rate (Cohn et al., 2009). A good practice is to employ mitigation strategies when breaking bad news to the user (Brown and Levinson, 1987; Fraser, 1980), e.g. by presenting obligations as options (Williams, 2011), or presenting the "bad news" simultaneously with "good news". We provide for discussion another requirement for interactive systems in this case: *The system must not produce ambiguously interpretable answers* – consider a catastrophic answer of "okay" as an affirmative response to a wrongly parsed utterance that was actually an expression of intent for suicide, a frequent phenomenon with risk patients (Kelly, 2009).

- **Borderline Personality Disorder:** This type of disorders, characterized by emotional instability, can lead to anxiety, social insecurity and depression, but also inappropriate outbursts of anger. Anger management techniques are employed to inhibit the expression of such anger (Swaffer and Hollin, 2009). An assistive system should be able to *cope with impulses of anger*, and as a bare minimum interrupt the interaction and offer to resume it at a later point. The EmoVoice system, for instance, can classify emotional features in natural language with good rates (Vogt et al., 2008), and could be used to identify anger.

- **Epilepsy:** Patients with acquired brain injuries frequently suffer from epilepsy. Even short (petit mal) epileptic seizures can lead to temporary absence and periods of confusion and disorientation (APA, 2000). In such a situation, the patient may utter irrational sentences or be silent altogether. An assistive system should be able to *detect these irrational deviations from* *the course of conversation*, and fill the user in again, abort the conversation, or call for help.

- **Panic:** Proneness to panic attacks can result from a multitude of afflictions and is hard to predict. In the event of a panicking interactant, the system should not take steps that could further exacerbate the situation. According to literature (Gournay and Denford, 2009), panic attacks are generally unable to do any real harm and subside quickly. Therefore, passivity from the system's side, in a neutral mode, is the minimal appropriate behavior. Panicking people are most likely not able to perform in interaction as successfully as usual – systems that should still be operable by a user in this situation must provide minimalistic shortcuts to essential features (i.e. a "panic button" for emergencies).

- **Anxiety:** Special care must be taken in the design of systems aimed at people with social anxiety. Interactants might be hesitant to open a conversation even with an artificial system. The system could take the initiative by simply opening with a short utterance about the task domain (Williams, 2011).

- **Phobias and Impulse Control Disorders:** Phobic disorders and obsessive-compulsive disorders can be triggered by environmental cues (Gournay and Denford, 2009). User interfaces have to take this into account, and *avoid presenting stimuli that could act as potential triggers* (e.g. people with an insect phobia should neither be presented with pictures of insects, nor their verbal mention). The same precautions are valid in the case of addictions.

Any interactive system, and in particular systems that do not only provide information but can also be made to perform tasks autonomously on behalf of the user, must be designed with all possible afflictions of all possible users in mind, not only as a wise legal precaution, but also as an ethical obligation to the designer. We argue that, quite unlike the 'best practices' of user interface design, there is no degree of optionality to the implementation of the above constraints and countermeasures, but that it must be performed with all musterable diligence. Some constraints are especially hard to meet in open-world systems (e.g. with free Internet access), since the contents presented are harder to predict.

Note that the set of conditions presented above is by no means comprehensive. For instance, we have, for now, altogether omitted an incorporation of autism-spectrum disorders or of functional psychoses such as schizophrenia, paraphrenia and paranoia – which are not uncommon in the older population (Ashton and Keady, 2009).

4 Summary

The VASA project is developing a multimodal natural-language agent-mediated assistance system for older people and patients with disabilities for enhancing their autonomy in the everyday tasks of communication and activity management. The clientele is afflicted with a variety of cognitive, psychic, and emotional conditions that have to be dealt with with extreme care and entail a necessity for specific safety mechanisms which will be implemented for VASA in coordination with the care personnel. We attempted to identify common conditions of older and impaired patients that should be considered and resolved in any assistive system (or indeed any autonomous interactive system) that might communicate with them. Factors that could lead to a detrimental outcome of such an interaction include depression, emotional instability, disorientation, panic, anxiety and phobia. Some constraints on the design rationale for such systems can provide a mitigation of those risks: avoiding ambiguity in the system's utterances, coping with anger, irrationality and panic by employing appropriate system responses, capability for system-side initiative, and preventing inadvertent stimulation of disorders. Since the field of potential interactants for generic assistive systems is vast, as any inspection of a larger health-care institution will show, more discussion in the research community should aim at establishing a stable ontology of their special needs and the ramifications for the design of careful assistive systems.

Acknowledgments

This research is supported by the Deutsche Forschungsgemeinschaft (DFG) in the Center of Excellence in Cognitive Interaction Technology (CITEC).

References

American Psychiatric Association. 2000. *Diagnostic and Statistical Manual of Mental Disorders DSM-IV-TR, Fourth Edition.* American Psychiatric Publishing, Inc., Arlington, VA.

Peter Ashton and John Keady. 2009. Mental disorders of older people. Newell & Gournay (eds.), *Mental Health Nursing: an Evidence-Based Approach*, 341–370. Churchill Livingstone, Philadelphia, PA.

Paul Brown and Stephen Levinson. 1987. *Politeness. Some Universals in Language Usage.* Cambridge University Press, Cambridge.

Jeffrey F. Cohn, Tomas Simon Kruez, Iain Matthews, Ying Yang, Minh Hoai Nguyen, Margara Tejera Padilla, Feng Zhou, and Fernando de la Torre. 2009. Detecting Depression from Facial Actions and Vocal Prosody. *Proceedings of the 3rd International Conference on Affective Computing and Intelligent Interaction and Workshops (ACII 2009)*, 1–7. IEEE, Amsterdam.

Susan K. Fager, David R. Beukelman, Tom Jakobs, and John-Paul Hosom. 2010. Evaluation of a Speech Recognition Prototype for Speakers with Moderate and Severe Dysarthria: A Preliminary Report *Augmentative and Alternative Communication*, 26(4):267-277.

Bruce Fraser. 1980. Conversational mitigation. *Journal of Pragmatics*, 4:341–350.

Kevin Gournay and Lindsay Denford. 2009. Phobias and Rituals. Newell & Gournay (eds.), *Mental Health Nursing: an Evidence-Based Approach*, 207–224. Churchill Livingstone, Philadelphia, PA.

Mark S. Hawley, Pam Enderby, Phil Green, Stuart Cunningham, Simon Brownsell, James Carmichael, Mark Parker, Athanassios Hatzis, Peter ONeill, and Rebecca Palmer. 2007. A speech-controlled environmental control system for people with severe dysarthria. *Medical Engineering & Physics*, 29(5):586–593.

Robert Gareth Hill and Geoff Shepherd. 2009. Disorders of Mood: Depression and Mania. Newell & Gournay (eds.), *Mental Health Nursing: an Evidence-Based Approach*, 165–185. Churchill Livingstone, Philadelphia, PA.

Cui Jian, Nadine Sasse, Nicole von Steinbüchel-Rheinwall, Frank Schafmeister, Hui Shi, Carsten Rachuy, and Holger Schmidt. 2011. Towards effective, efficient and elderly-friendly multimodal interaction. *Proceedings of the 4th International Conference on Pervasive Technologies Related to Assistive Environments (PETRA 2011)*, article 45, 1–8. ACM, New York, NY.

Sarah Kelly. 2009. Suicide and Self-Harm. Newell & Gournay (eds.), *Mental Health Nursing: an Evidence-Based Approach*, 187–206. Churchill Livingstone, Philadelphia, PA.

Parimala Raghavendra, Elisabet Rosengren, and Sheri Hunnicutt. 2001. An investigation of different degrees of dysarthric speech as input to speaker-adaptive and speaker-dependent recognition systems. *Augmentative and Alternative Communication*, 17(4):265-275.

Benjamin J. Sadock, Harold I. Kaplan, and Virginia A. Sadock. 2007. *Kaplan & Sadock's Synopsis of Psychiatry: Behavioral Sciences/Clinical Psychiatry.* Lippincott Williams & Wilkins, Philadelphia.

Tracey Swaffer and Clive R. Hollin. 2009. Anger and Impulse Control. Newell & Gournay (eds.), *Mental Health Nursing: an Evidence-Based Approach*, 267–289. Churchill Livingstone, Philadelphia, PA.

Ravichander Vipperla, Maria Wolters, Kallirroi Georgila, and Steve Renals. 2009. Speech input from older users in smart environments: Challenges and perspectives. *HCI (6): Universal Access in Human-Computer Interaction, Intelligent and Ubiquitous Interaction Environments* , LNCS 5615:117–126. Springer, Heidelberg.

Thurid Vogt, Elisabeth André, and Nikolaus Bee. 2008. EmoVoice - A framework for online recognition of emotions from voice. *Proceedings of the 4th IEEE tutorial and research workshop on Perception and Interactive Technologies for Speech-Based Systems (PIT 2008)*, 188–199. Springer, Heidelberg.

Val Williams. 2011. *Disability and discourse : analysing inclusive conversation with people with intellectual disabilities.* Wiley-Blackwell, Chichester, West Sussex / Malden, MA.

World Health Organization. 2001. *International Classification of Functioning, Disability and Health: ICF*, WHO, Geneva, Switzerland.

Maria Wolters, Kallirroi Georgila, Johanna D. Moore, and Sarah E. MacPherson. 2009. Being Old Doesn't Mean Acting Old: How Older Users Interact with Spoken Dialog Systems. *ACM Transactions on Accessible Computing (TACCESS)*, 2(1):1–39.

Ramin Yaghoubzadeh and Stefan Kopp. 2011. Creating familiarity through adaptive behavior generation in human-agent interaction. *Proceedings of the 11th International Conference on Intelligent Virtual Agents (IVA 2011)*, LNCS(LNAI) 6895:195–201. Springer, Heidelberg.

Victoria Young and Alex Mihailidis. 2010. Difficulties in Automatic Speech Recognition of Dysarthric Speakers and Implications for Speech-Based Applications Used by the Elderly: A Literature Review. *Assistive Technology*, 22(2):99–112.

Speech and Gesture Interaction in an Ambient Assisted Living Lab

Dimitra Anastasiou
SFB/TR8 Spatial Cognition,
Languages Science,
University of Bremen,
Germany
anastasiou@uni-bremen.de

Cui Jian
SFB/TR8 Spatial Cognition,
University of Bremen,
Germany
ken@informatik.uni-bremen.de

Desislava Zhekova
Department of Linguistics,
Indiana University, USA
dzhekova@indiana.edu

Abstract

In this paper we describe our recent and future research on multimodal interaction in an Ambient Assisted Living Lab. Our work combines two interaction modes, speech and gesture, for multiple device control in Ambient Assisted Living environments. We conducted a user study concerning multimodal interaction between participants and an intelligent wheelchair in a smart home environment. Important empirical data were collected through the user study, which encouraged further developments on our multi-modal interactive system for Ambient Assisted Living environments.

1 Introduction

Multimodal interaction has been gaining more and more importance in various application systems and domains. On one hand, it is considered as an encouraging way to improve the effectiveness and efficiency of interaction in general, and on the other hand, to increase user satisfaction in a more natural and intuitive manner (Jaimes & Sebe, 2007; Oviatt, 1999).

Meanwhile, the domain of Ambient Assisted Living (AAL), although very significantly and increasingly well researched in recent literature (Steg et al., 2006; Fuchsberger, 2008; Wichert & Eberhardt, 2011), has not been enriched with profuse advanced multimodal technologies so far. Therefore, generally as well as particularly in assistive environments, multimodal applications are not only preferred, but also often the only solution for people who cannot master their everyday tasks by themselves. These multimodal applications are showing their necessities of compensating for the various visual, perceptual, sensory, cognitive, and motoric impairments of senior and/or disabled people.

We focus on speech and gesture as two intuitive modalities which can be combined to compensate for physical and/or cognitive limitations; speech interaction for those who have motor disabilities and gesture for those with speech impairments. A Wizard-of-Oz (WoZ)-controlled user study concerning multimodal interaction between participants and an intelligent wheelchair took place in our AAL lab. A drawback in the design of gesture-based user interfaces today is the lack of experience and empirical data about which gestures are required for which activities. Our goal in the presented user study is to collect empirical speech and gesture data of natural dialogue in Human-Robot Interaction (HRI).

This paper is laid out as follows: in section 2 we present the most relevant work on speech interaction in assistive environments (2.1), spatial gestures in assistive environments (2.2) and speech-gesture interaction (2.3). Section 3 gives an introduction to our Ambient Assisted Living Lab and the intelligent wheelchair. Section 4 describes the current speech interaction with the wheelchair in our assistive environment/smart home. Section 5 reports on a user study focusing on the speech-gesture interaction within this environment. Conclusion and future work follow in section 6.

2 Related Work

One of the main goals of AAL is to alleviate and compensate for the disabilities of its inhabitants. The latter are often predisposed to constant and permanent increase of their inability to orally express themselves and/or adequately employ elementary motoric functions. Thus, efficient and dynamic interaction of the AAL modalities should be targeted in order to balance the lack of either eloquence and/or movement. In case further deficiencies are present, additional modalities that can account for those deficiencies should be considered. For example, if a person experiences any kind of speech disorder, the speech modality can be exchanged with a typed-text interface. Yet, in the following subsections we will concentrate on related work about two common interaction modalities, speech and gesture, and the way they can interact with each other.

2.1 Speech interaction in assistive environments

As one of the most important interaction modalities in assistive environments, there has been a significant amount of research on speech interaction regarding different kinds of motivation and technology-dependent approaches.

Some studies are focusing on gathering objective and subjective evidence for motivating and supporting further development on speech interaction. Takahashi et al. (2003) collected dialogue examples and conducted a recognition experiment for the collected speech; Ivanecky et al. (2011) found that the set of the commands for the house control is relatively small (usually around 50).

At the same time, other research concerning general-purpose speech-enabled dialogue systems has also been reported. Goetze et al. (2010) described technologies for acoustic user interaction in AAL scenarios, where they designed and evaluated a multimedia reminding and calendar system. The authors carried out an automatic speech recognition (ASR) performance study having as training set both male and female speakers of different age and hearing loss. The results showed that the ASR performance was lower for older persons and for female. Moreover, Becker et al. (2009) carried out experiments in an assistive environment using voice recognition and pointed out that "the speech interface is the easiest way for the user to interact with the computer-based service system".

Furthermore, much effort has been put into considering the special requirements of assistive environments and developing the accordingly adapted interactive systems. Krajewski et al. (2008) described an acoustic framework for detecting accident-prone fatigue states according to prosody, articulation and speech quality related speech characteristics for speech-based human computer interaction (HCI). Moreover, Jian et al. (2012) studied, implemented, and evaluated the speech interface of a multimodal interactive guidance system based on the most common elderly-centered characteristics during interaction within assistive environments.

2.2 Spatial gestures in assistive environments

We coin the term "spatial" to describe gestures that often iconically represent spatial concepts (Rauscher et al., 1996). Alibali (2005: 307) states: "gestures contribute to effective communication of spatial information". She added that "speakers tend to produce gestures when they produce linguistic units that contain spatial information, and they gesture more when talking about spatial topics than when talking about abstract or verbal ones". Kopp (2005) has shown that gestures have sufficient specificity to be communicative of spatial information. Spatial gestures belong to *representational* gestures, which according to McNeill's (1992) taxonomy can be deictic, iconic, or metaphoric. Kita (2009: 145) stated: "representational gestures (...) that express spatial contents (…) reflect the cognitive differences in how direction, relative location and different axes in space are conceptualized and processed".

As far as spatial gestures in assistive environments is concerned, Nazemi et al. (2011) conducted an experiment, where test subjects in middle age were asked to make gestures with the *WiiMote* to scroll, zoom, renew, and navigate in a relational database. The results showed that in complex tasks, participants employed more and various gestures. Neßelrath et al. (2011) designed a gesture-based system for context-sensitive interaction with a smart kitchen. Users had to solve interaction tasks by controlling appliances in a smart home. Recently Marinc et al. (2012) presented a demonstrator that uses *Kinect* to recognize pointing gestures for device selection and control. When a device is selected, a graphical user interface (GUI) is shown on a screen to inform the user that the interaction has started. A hand movement to the left stops the HCI.

2.3 Speech-gesture interaction

Concerning speech accompaniment of gestures, Chovil (1992), among others, stated that speakers frequently use gesture to supplement speech. McNeill (1992) pointed out that speech and gesture must cooperate to express a person's meaning and Goldin-Meadow (2003) stated that speech-associated gestures often convey information that complements the information conveyed in the talk they accompany and, in this sense, are meaningful. Similarly, Kendon (2004) suggests that gestures enrich the speech, helping the interlocutor to easily express concepts that will otherwise be complex to explain through speech only. McNeill (2000) points out that gestures and the synchronous speech are semantically and pragmatically co-expressive.

Specifically concerning the relationship between spatial gestures and speech, Kita (2000) stated that a possible function of gesture is that gesture may help speakers to package spatial information into units suitable for verbal output. Moreover, Hostetter & Alibali (2005) regarded individual differences in gesture and found that the gesture rate was highest among individuals who had a combination of high spatial skill and low verbal skill.

Furthermore, research has been carried out towards a grammar of gesture, in other words the relationship of gestures within a multimodal grammar. Fricke (2009) claimed that in German spoken language, co-speech gestures can be structurally integrated as constituents of nominal phrases, and can semantically modify the nucleus of the nominal phrases. Hahn & Rieser (2010) looked at the types of gestures co-occurring with noun phrases and their function, semantic values, and how these values interface with a natural language expression.

In addition, the employment of gesture to improve the semantic analysis of the dialogues in AAL has gained considerable attention in the research community in the last decade. In particular the effect of gesture on the improvement of co-reference resolution (the process of determining if two phrases in a discourse refer to the same real-world entity) has been examined in a variety of studies. Eisenstein and Davis (2006) consider various gesture features and delineate their importance for the co-reference process. Chen et. al. (2011) show that when the pronominal mentions are typed and simultaneously a pointing gesture is used, the co-reference performance improves for personal and deictic pronouns. Co-reference in spoken dialogues has proven to be much more different than the one we encounter in written texts. As Strube and Müller (2003) point out, a big number of the pronouns used in spoken dialogue have non-noun phrase (NP) antecedents or no antecedents at all, which can prove to be a challenge for the semantic analysis of dialogue in AAL. The TRAINS93 corpus study of Byron and Allen (1998) shows that about 50% of the pronouns that are used in the corpus have antecedents that are non-NP-phrases. Thus, co-reference resolution for dialogue can highly benefit from the additional information that various modalities and more specifically gesture can provide.

3 Our Ambient Assisted Living Lab and the Intelligent Wheelchair

The Bremen Ambient Assisted Living Lab (BAALL) comprises all necessary conditions for trial living intended for two persons. This lab is a smart home suitable for the elderly and people with disabilities. It has an area of $60m^2$ and contains all standard living areas, i.e. kitchen, bathroom, bedroom, and living room. It has intelligent adaptable household appliances and furniture for compensating for special limitations, e.g. separate kitchen cabinets can be moved up and down. The lab looks like a normal apartment and the technological infrastructure is discreet, if visible at all.

In the lab mobility assistance is provided through an *Intelligent Wheelchair* as well as an *Intelligent Walker*. For our studies we use the autonomous wheelchair/robot which is equipped with two laser range-sensors, wheel encoders, and an onboard computer; the wheelchair has a spoken dialogue

interface that allows to navigate to predefined destinations and to control devices in the lab.
The goal of the smart environment with mobility assistants and smart furniture is to evaluate new ambient assisted living technologies regarding their everyday usability. Users can interact through various interaction modes, such as a head joystick, a touch screen, and natural language dialogue.
In this paper we focus on the natural language dialogue and on contact-free, touchless, and not pen-based gestures in interaction with the wheelchair and smart furniture.
Figure 1 shows a smart appliance, i.e. the kitchen cabinet, which is moving down, so that it can be reachable for the wheelchair user.

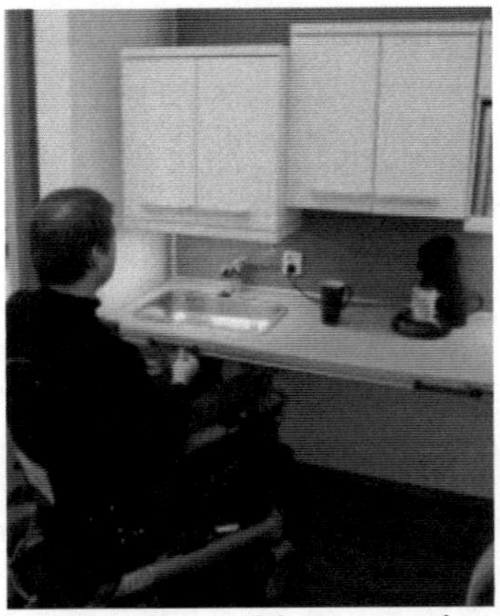

Figure 1. Kitchen cabinets moving down

4 Speech Interaction in our Lab

Since the users of an AAL environment are typically untrained persons, elderly persons or persons possibly with physical or cognitive deficits, the user-centered analysis and adaptation of specific AAL-related application scenarios are necessary for developing a speech-enabled interactive dialogue system for our environment. In the following subsections we first describe the speech-related functionalities for the targeted users in our smart home (4.1) and then report on our recent work at the grammar level for improving the common problems caused by the automatic speech recognition (4.2).

4.1 Speech-related functionalities

According to the various assistance possibilities currently provided in our AAL environment, each of the speech supportive functionalities can be classified based on the following three levels:

- An **explicit elementary action** on behalf of a simple dialogic utterance is used to ask for a specific assisting service to control each device in the AAL environment, such as "turn on the kitchen light", "close the door of the bathroom" or "drive me to my bed", etc.
- An **implicit composite action**, which can be uttered by simple or longer sentences, is used to converse with the dialogue system to trigger a set of explicit elementary actions regarding a predefined yet dynamically adaptable planning component. A typical utterance of such is "where is my pizza?", which can then result in a sequence of actions including driving the user to the kitchen, opening all the doors on the path, showing the location of the pizza either orally or using other already implemented hardware supports (e.g. blinking light).
- A **context sensitive negotiating action**, which can be uttered during a clarification situation, should be used on the top of the explicit and implicit actions according to the situated context. Our AAL environment is in fact a multi-agent environment, which involves necessary dialogic interaction with other agents and their activities with respect to the possible temporal and spatial conflicts. For example, if a user wants to bake a pizza and the system detects that the oven is being used, the system would inform the user about it, then the user should be allowed to say "then take me to the oven when it's available".

In order to support the above three speech-enabled dialogic activities, a general dialogue system framework, the Diaspace Adaptive Information State Interaction Executive (DAISIE, cf. Ross & Bateman, 2009), is investigated and accordingly being extended.
DAISIE is a tightly coupled information state-based (see Larsson & Traum, 2000) dialogue backbone that fuses a formal language based dialogue controller, which provides a complex yet easily reusable plug-in mechanism for domain specific applications. Figure 2 depicts the general architecture of DAISIE.

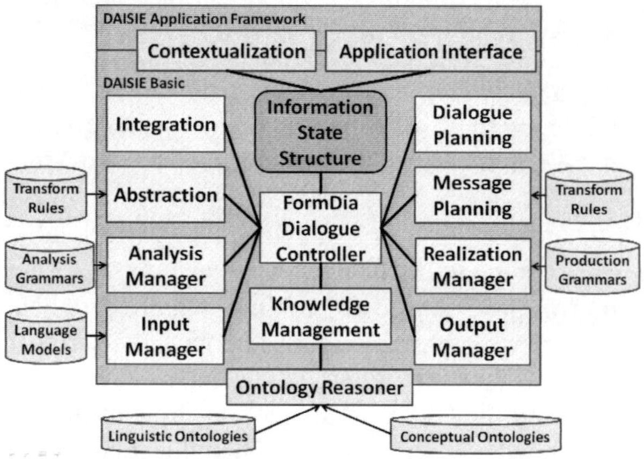

Figure 2. DAISIE with its plug-in components

According to the requirements of an operational dialogue system, the DAISIE architecture consists of a set of principle processing components, which are classified into the following three functionality groups:

- *The DAISIE Plug-ins* include a range of common language technology resources, such as speech recognizers/synthesizers, language parsers/generators, etc.
- *The DAISIE Basic System* integrates all the DAISIE plug-ins with the information state structure, knowledge monument component and the formal language based dialogue controller into a basic functional dialogue system.
- *The DAISIE Application Framework* specifies the application dependent components and provides a direct interface between the concrete domain application and the DAISIE basic system.

An instantiation of DAISIE is being developed and tested, which includes the implementation ranging over all levels of linguistic and conceptual representation and reasoning, as well as the adaptation of the current hybrid unified dialogue model (cf. Shi et al., 2011) to the AAL environment application regarding the listed three speech-related activities and possibly further modalities, such as gesture (see section 5).

4.2 Foot-syllable Grammar

Reliable speech recognition is a key factor for the success of a dialogue system in our AAL environment. Currently, the expression stratum of the language system is modeled with two components in the *DAISIE* Framework: a speech recognizer for understanding spoken text and speech synthesizer for producing it. We use VoCon[1] as our speech recognizer, which takes a restriction grammar to know which commands the AAL and the wheelchair can undertake.

A foot-syllable restriction grammar was developed for optimized performance (Couto Vale & Mast, 2012). This grammar has a three-level structure starting at the lowest level with the syllable (S), an intermediate structure named *foot* (F), and the clause (C). A foot is a rhythmic unit in the compositional hierarchy of spoken language, which contains syllables as its parts and which is part of a curve (Halliday & Matthiessen, 2004). In German, it is composed by one stressed syllable and its adjacent unstressed ones. Below we present a segment of the grammar:

```
Foot-Syllable Grammar
<Foot1>      : <IndIBegin> <kYStrong> <CEWeak> ;
<IndIBegin> : <InWeak> <dIWeak> | <IWeak> <nIWeak> ;
<kYStrong>  : 'kY !pronounce("'kY") ;
<CEWeak>    : CE !pronounce("CE") | C$ !pronounce ("C$") ;
<IWeak>     : I  !pronounce("I")  | $  !pronounce ("$")  ;
<InWeak>    : In !pronounce("In") | $n !pronounce ("$n") ;
<nIWeak>    : nI !pronounce("nI") | n$ !pronounce ("n$") ;
<dIWeak>    : dI !pronounce("dI") | d$ !pronounce ("d$") ;
```

The foot-syllable grammar (FS) was contrasted with a foot-word (FW) and a phrase-word grammar (PW) in speech recognition effectiveness. The foot helped enforce corpus-based restrictions on syntactic structures and the syllable gave fine control over phonological variation. We conducted an evaluation study and our results have shown that, for complex highly flexible natural language dialogue situations such as human-robot interaction in AAL, a restriction grammar such as our foot-syllable grammar outperforms the other two approaches: 51,81% (FS) of correctly recognized utterances versus 26,67% (FW) and 6,67% (PW). We argue that using phonological units, such as syllables and foot units, provides a better way to achieve high recognition performance than phrases and words in both development cost and effectiveness.

[1] http://www.nuance.com/for-business/by-product/automotive-products-services/vocon3200/index.htm, 19/03/2012

5 Speech-Gesture User Study

A user study was conducted in our lab in November-December 2011. This user study included a real-life everyday scenario of a human user using a wheelchair to navigate in their environment by means of speech and gesture. The goal was to observe whether people would gesture and how, and what they would say if they used a wheelchair in their domotic environment. The study took place in BAALL and 20 German participants (students) took part in the study (mean age 25). Older users were not considered as participants in this study, as various tests, such as OsteoArthritis screening, neuropsychological tests, memory tests etc. would have to be taken in order to make sure that the elderly are physically able of performing gestures. Furthermore, it is difficult to bring seniors to the lab due to their physical condition. Elderly users might also be digitally intimidated by such technology. Although the tested group and the prospective user group are divergent, our user study primarily focuses on the collection of empirical gesture-speech data through the interaction of participants with technical devices in a smart home and thus does not distinguish between participants based on their age.

The participants were asked to act as if they were dependent on the wheelchair called *Rolland*. They had to navigate with *Rolland* to carry out daily activities (wash their teeth, eat something, read a book). They were informed in advance about the goal of the study, i.e. the collection of speech-gesture data and the video recording. The participants used a Bluetooth head-set and their activities were recorded by two digital IP cameras placed in BAALL, and also an SLR camera on *Rolland*'s back. Through audio and video streaming an experimenter (WoZ) selected through a GUI the destination point of *Rolland*. It is important to note again that we are interested into collecting various empirical spoken commands and gestures produced by the participants in their interaction with the wheelchair during the experimental run. Thus both the wheelchair navigation and *Rolland*'s speech feedback were WoZ-controlled. During most of the tasks the user was sitting on the wheelchair, but in one task the wheelchair drove autonomously without the user, as differences in gesture may change based on the recipient (see discussion in Rimé & Schiaratura, 1991). Technical problems appeared in 8 sessions out of 20, when *Rolland* did not drive to the desired destination. The reasons for this are outside the scope of our research and of this paper. We evaluated 12 sessions regarding speech, but all 20 sessions regarding gesture.

As far as the results of this study are concerned, we collected 317 spoken commands in total. Many different language variants were uttered in order to carry out the same task. For example, four distinct utterances which were produced when participants were sitting on the bed and asked *Rolland* to come to them follow:

i) "Rolland, komm her"
(Rolland, come here)

ii) "Rolland, <break9secs> Rolland, <break3secs> komm her"
(Rolland, Rolland, come here)

iii) "Rolland, komm bitte zum Bett, hier wo ich sitze"
(Rolland, please come to the bed, here where I am sitting)

iv) "Rolland, fahr zum Bett"
(Rolland, drive to the bed)

Thus many context-sensitive utterances appeared in the collected data; for example, in the first two utterances above the participants did not use the name of a landmark (*bed*) in their command. Moreover, in the second example above we see that the participant waited for a backchannel feedback from the wheelchair and then uttered the actual command (*come here*).

From the study also the attitude, e.g. politeness, and expectations of the participants against the robot were measured. The style, volume of utterance, waiting time for the wheelchair to react as well as the sentence structure and lexical content were measurement factors. For example, male participants used more direct style with imperative sentences than female and included the name of their wheelchair in their command.

Concerning gestural frequency during the user study, in 7 sessions out of 20 participants employed at least one gesture during a session. In 6 sessions participants used deictic/pointing gestures and in 1 an iconic gesture (rubbing hands under the tap to represent washing hands). In 2 of the 7 sessions participants gestured more than once, while in the remaining 5 sessions, they gestured

once. The participants gestured mostly when something happened out of order, e.g. the wheelchair drove to a wrong place or stopped too far from the participant. Particularly in the bathroom, the wheelchair could not drive very close to the washbasin (predefined destination) and thus many participants gestured so that the wheelchair moves closer.
Two exceptions on gestural types and frequency were the following: in one case a male participant used often iconic gestures "for fun", e.g. representing that he holds a gun. Another participant (female) gestured constantly using pointing gestures during all activities that she carried out. These cases can be attributed to personal influences, e.g. the user's personality (see Rehm et al., 2008).
The gestures are annotated with the tool ANVIL (Kipp et al. 2007), a free video annotation tool that offers multi-layered annotation. The gesture annotation conventions for gesture, form, space, and trajectory, which are based on the practice of N. Furuyama (see McNeill, 2005: 273-278), are followed.
As far as co-reference is concerned, in all 317 commands there were several instances that the participants employed in their utterances. Yet, all of them were either references to the participant him/herself or to the wheelchair:

i) "*Rolland*, drehe dich bitte um"
(*Rolland, turn around please*)
ii) "Fahr mich bitte zum Badezimmer"
(*Drive me to the bathroom please*)

For those cases, the participants did not use gestures. We assume that the rare use of co-reference in our user study is due to the fact that participants almost never had to refer to the same entity again. Once a command was uttered, the WoZ executed the required action and the participants could move further to the next task they had in their agendas. Thus, once an entity (i.e. the sofa, the bathroom, the kitchen) has been introduced, the participants never needed to refer back to that same entity again.
Last but not least, nobody of the participants realized that the experiment was WoZ, believing that the wheelchair moved based on their own commands.

6 Conclusion and Future Work

Our lab is equipped with intelligent adaptable household appliances and furniture for compensating for special limitations; this lab can be used as an experiment area for many user studies with different purposes.
In the presented user study we collected empirical speech and gesture data of natural dialogue in HRI. By making the speech-gesture interaction between users and robot more natural, intuitive, effective, efficient, and user-friendly, assistive environments will become more appropriate in the real world used by seniors and/or *seniors to be*, people actively planning their future.
A planned second user study handles selection and control of objects in a smart environment. In this study objects such as television, lights, electronic sliding doors, etc. will be remotely controlled by the experimenter (WoZ). The participants will be requested to select objects and control their position and level (higher, louder, etc.). A condition tested here will be the presence/lack of ambiguity. Participants will be asked to "open a door" or "turn on a light" having many doors and lights available in the lab. In addition, the wheelchair will be intentionally driven by an experimenter to a wrong destination or stopped on its way to a destination point. This adjustment has been made considering the results in the conducted study that participants gestured more when something went wrong.
A third study is planned in order to identify which spatial gestures are universal and which are *locale-dependent*. Within the field of localization, *locale* is a combination of language and culture. The criteria of *locale* selection are countries with i) big geographic distance, ii) strong cultural differences, iii) diversity of gestures based on literature evidence, and iv) typologically different languages. This study is necessary to investigate the differences in speech-gesture interaction between the German and other *locales*.
Last but not least, a small scale follow-up study with elderly people will take place in a nursing home. There the elderly could be requested to perform gestures that have already been collected in our previous studies in order to evaluate them depending on their skills and preferences.
The collected data from the user studies stored in a corpus will be examined based on the speech-

gesture alignment concerning their semantics, their temporal arrangement, and their coordinated organization in the phrasal structure. Later an extension for the semantics of gesture types will be added to the Generalized Upper Model (GUM) in order to anchor spatial gestures into a semantic spatial representation. GUM (Bateman et al., 2010) is a linguistically motivated ontology for the semantics of spatial language of German and English. New GUM categories will be created for gestures, when the linguistic ones are not applicable and/or sufficient.

Acknowledgments

We gratefully acknowledge the support of the Deutsche Forschungsgemeinschaft (DFG) through the Collaborative Research Center SFB/TR 8 Spatial Cognition. We also thank Daniel Vale, Bernd Gersdorf, Thora Tenbrink, Carsten Gendorf, and Vivien Mast for their help with the user study.

References

M. Alibali. 2005. Gesture in spatial cognition: expressing, communicating, and thinking about spatial information. Spatial Cognition and Computation, 5(4):307-331.

J. Bateman, J. Hois, R. Ross, and T. Tenbrink. 2010. A linguistic ontology of space for natural language processing. Artificial Intelligence, 174(14): 1027-1071.

E. Becker, Z. Le, K. Park, Y. Lin and F. Makedon. 2009. Event-based experiments in an assistive environment using wireless sensor networks and voice recognition. Proceedings of the International conference on *Pervasive* technologies for assistive environments (PETRA).

D.K. Byron and J.F. Allen. 1998. Resolving demonstrative pronouns in the TRAINS93 corpus. New Approaches to Discourse Anaphora: Proceedings of the 2nd Colloquium on Discourse Anaphora and Anaphor Resolution (DAARC2), 68-81.

L. Chen, A. Wang and B. Di Eugenio, B. 2011. Improving pronominal and deictic co-reference resolution with multi-modal features. Proceedings of the SIGDIAL Conference, 307-311.

N. Chovil. 1992. Discourse-oriented facial displays in conversation. Research on Language and Social Interaction, 25:163-194.

D. Couto Vale and V. Mast. 2012. Customizing Speech Recognizers for Situated Dialogue Systems. Proceedings of the 15th International Conference on Text, Speech and Dialogue.

J. Eisenstein and R. Davis. 2006. Gesture improves coreference resolution. Proceedings of the Human Language Technology Conference of the NAACL, 37-40.

E. Fricke. 2009. Multimodal attribution: How gestures are syntactically integrated into spoken language. Proceedings of GESPIN: Gesture and Speech in Interaction.

V. Fuchsberger. 2008. Ambient assisted living: elderly people's needs and how to face them. Proceedings of the 1st ACM International Workshop on Semantic Ambient Media Experiences, 21-24.

S. Goetze, N. Moritz, J.E. Appell, M. Meis, C. Bartsch and J. Bitzer. 2010. Acoustic user interfaces for ambient-assisted living technologies. Inform Health Soc Care, 35(3-4):125-143.

S. Goldin-Meadow. 2003. Hearing gesture: How our hands help us think. Cambridge, MA: Harvard University Press.

F. Hahn and H. Rieser. 2010. Explaining speech gesture alignment in MM dialogue using gesture typology. P. Lupowski and M. Purver (Eds.), Proceedings of the 14th Workshop on the Semantics and Pragmatics of Dialogue (SemDial), 99-111.

F.M.A.K. Halliday and C.M.I.M. Matthiessen 2004. An introduction to functional grammar. 3rd Edition. Edward Arnold, London.

A. Hostetter and M. Alibali. 2005. Raise your hand if you're spatial–Relations between verbal and spatial skills and gesture production. Gesture, 7(1): 73-95.

J. Ivanecky, S. Mehlhase and M. Mieskes, M. 2011. An Intelligent House Control Using Speech Recognition with Integrated Localization. R. Wichert and B. Eberhardt, B. (Eds.), 4. AAL Kongress. Berlin, Germany.

A. Jaimes and N. Sebe. 2007. Multimodal human-computer interaction: A Survey, Computational Vision and Image Understanding. Elsevier Science Inc., New York, USA, 116-134.

C. Jian, F. Schafmeister, C. Rachuy, N. Sasse, H. Shi, H. Schmidt and N.v. Steinbüchel. 2012. Evaluating a Spoken Language Interface of a Multimodal Interactive Guidance System for Elderly Persons. Proceedings of the International Conference on Health Informatics.

A. Kendon. 2004. Gesture: Visible action as utterance. Cambridge: Cambridge University Press.

S. Kita. 2000. How representational gestures help speaking. McNeill, D. (Ed.), Language and gesture, Cambridge, UK: Cambridge University Press, 162-185.

S. Kita. 2009. Cross-cultural variation of speech-accompanying gesture: A review. Language and Cognitive Processes, 24(2): 145-167.

M. Kipp, M. Neff and I. Albrecht. 2007. An annotation scheme for conversational gestures: How to economically capture timing and form. Language Resources and Evaluation Journal, 41: 325-339.

S. Kopp. 2005. The spatial specificity of iconic gestures. Proceedings of the 7th International Conference of the German Cognitive Science Society, 112-117.

J. Krajewski, R., Wieland and A. Batliner. 2008. An acoustic Framework for detecting Fatique in Speech based Human Computer Interaction. Proceedings of the 11th International Conference on Computers Help People with Special Needs, 54-61.

S. Larsson and D. Traum. 2000. Information State and Dialogue Management in the TRINDI Dialogue Move Engine Toolkit. Natural Language Engineering. Special Issue on Best Practice in Spoken Language Dialogue Systems Engineering, 323-340.

A. Marinc, C. Stocklöw and S. Tazari, S. 2012. 3D Interaktion in AAL Umgebungen basierend auf Ontologien. Proceedings of AAL Kongress.

D. McNeill. 1992. Hand and Mind: What Gestures reveal about Thought. University of Chicago Press.

D. McNeill. 2000. Introduction. McNeill, D. (Ed.), Language and gesture. Cambridge: Cambridge University Press.

D. McNeill. 2005. Gestures and Thought. University of Chicago Press.

K. Nazemi, D. Burkhardt, C. Stab, M. Breyer, R. Wichert and D.W. Fellner. 2011. Natural gesture interaction with accelerometer-based devices in ambient assisted environments. R. Wichert and B. Eberhardt, B. (Eds.), 4. AAL-Kongress, Springer, 75-84.

R. Neßelrath, C. Lu, C.H. Schulz, J., Frey, and J. Alexandersson. 2011. A gesture based system for context-sensitive interaction with smart homes. R. Wichert and B. Eberhardt, B. (Eds.), 4. AAL-Kongress, 209-222.

S. T. Oviatt. 1999. Ten myths of multimodal interaction. Communications of the ACM. ACM New York, USA, 42(11): 74-81.

F.H. Rauscher, R.M. Krauss and Y. Chen. 1996. Gesture, speech, and lexical access: The role of lexical movements in speech production. Psychological Science, 7: 226-230.

M. Rehm, N. Bee and E., André. 2008. Wave like an Egyptian: accelerometer-based gesture recognition for culture specific interactions. Proceedings of the 2nd British HCI Group Annual Conference on People and Computers: Culture, Creativity, Interaction, 1:13-22.

B. Rimé and L. Schiaratura. 1991. Gesture and speech. Fundamentals of nonverbal behavior. Studies in emotion & social interaction, 239-281.

J. R. Ross and J. Bateman. 2009. Daisie: Information State Dialogues for Situated Systems. Proceedings of Text, Speech and Dialogue, 5729/2009, 379-386.

H. Shi, C. Jian and C. Rachuy. 2011. Evaluation of a Unified Dialogue Model for Human-Computer Interaction. International Journal of Computational Linguistics and Applications, 2.

H. Steg, H. Strese, C. Loroff, J. Hull and S. Schmidt. 2006. Europe is facing a demographic challenge ambient assisted living offers solutions. VDI/VDE/IT, Berlin, Germany.

M. Strube and C. Müller. 2003. A machine learning approach to pronoun resolution in spoken dialogue. Proceedings of the 41st Annual Meeting on Association for Computational Linguistics, 1:168-175.

S. Takahashi, T. Morimoto, S. Maeda and N. Tsuruta. 2003. Dialogue experiment for elderly people in home health care system. Proceedings of the 6th International Conference on Text, Speech and Dialogue, 418-423.

R. Wichert and B. Eberhardt, B. (Eds.). 2011. Ambient Assisted Living. 4. AAL-Kongress, Springer.

Reduction of Non-stationary Noise for a Robotic Living Assistant using Sparse Non-negative Matrix Factorization

Benjamin Cauchi [1], **Stefan Goetze** [1], **Simon Doclo** [1,2]
[1]Fraunhofer Institute for Digital Media Technology (IDMT), Project group Hearing, Speech and Audio Technology (HSA), 26129 Oldenburg, Germany
[2]University of Oldenburg, Signal Processing group, 26129 Oldenburg, Germany
{benjamin.cauchi,s.goetze,simon.doclo}@idmt.fraunhofer.de

Abstract

Due to the demographic changes, support by means of assistive systems will become inevitable for home care and in nursing homes. Robot systems are promising solutions but their value has to be acknowledged by the patients and the care personnel. Natural and intuitive human-machine interfaces are an essential feature to achieve acceptance of the users. Therefore, automatic speech recognition (ASR) is a promising modality for such assistive devices. However, noises produced during movement of robots can degrade the ASR performances. This work focuses on noise reduction by a non-negative matrix factorization (NMF) approach to efficiently suppress non stationary noise produced by the sensors of an assisting robot system.

1 Introduction

The amount of older people in today's societies constantly grows due to demographic changes (European Commision Staff, 2007). Technical systems become more and more common to support for routine tasks of care givers or to assist older persons living alone in their home environments (Alliance, 2009). Various technical assistive systems have been developed recently (Lisetti et al., 2003), ranging from reminder systems (Boll et al., 2010; Goetze et al., 2010) to assisting robots (Chew et al., 2010; Goetze et al., 2012). If robot systems are supposed to navigate autonomously they usually rely on vision sensors (Aragon-Camarasa et al., 2010) or acoustic sensors (Youssef et al.,). Acoustic signals are usually picked up by microphones mounted on the robot. In real-world scenarios not only the desired signal part is picked up by these microphones as presented in Figure 1.

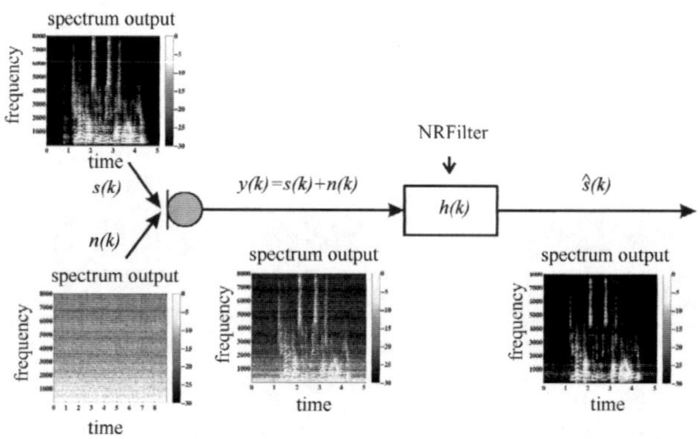

Figure 1: General denoising scheme

The desired signal part is usually superposed with disturbing noise originating from the environment or the robot system itself. This disturbance has to be removed from the microphone signal before it can be further processed, e.g. for navigation, position estimation, acoustic event detection, speaker detection or automatic speech recognition. This contribution focuses on acoustic input for a robot system and more specifically on the noise reduction preprocessing which is needed to clean up noisy sound signals.

Automatic speech recognition (Huang et al., 2001; Wölfel et al., 2009) is a convenient way to interact with robot assistants since speech is the most natural form of communication. However, to ensure acceptance of speech recognition systems a sufficiently high recognition rate has to be achieved (Pfister and T., 2008). Today's speech recognition systems succeed in achieving this recognition rate for environments with low amount of noise and reverberation. Unfortunately, while moving, robots can produce noise degrading the reliability of the ASR.

This work focuses on a specific application, suppressing the non stationary noise produced by the ultra-sonic sensors of a robotic assistant while moving. Please note that although in theory ultrasonic sensors do not produce sound disturbances in the audible range, artefacts due to the fast activation and deactivation of the sensors are present in the audible range and are clearly perceivable as a disturbance in the picked up microphone signal as shown later in Figure 6.

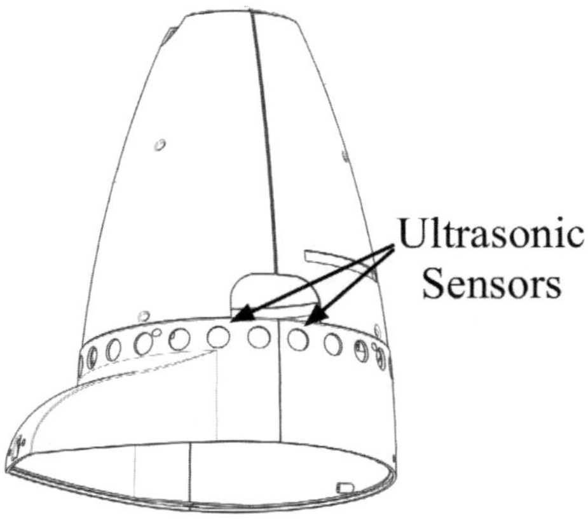

Figure 2: Lower part of the robot with ultrasonic sensors (Metralabs, 2010).

Non-negative Matrix Factorization (NMF) is an approach introduced by Lee & Seung (Lee and Seung, 2001) in which the data is described as the product of a set of basis and of a set of activation coefficients both being non-negative. We will apply the NMF approach to remove the disturbances caused by the ultrasonic sensors from the microphone input signal in the following. NMF and its various extensions have been proven efficient in sources separation (Cichocki et al., ; Virtanen, 2007), supervised detection of acoustic events (Cotton and Ellis, 2011) or to wind noise reduction (Schmidt et al.,). As the NMF algorithm can be fed with prior information about the content to identify, it is a handy way to suppress the non stationary noise produced by the sensors of the considered robotic assistant.

The remainder of this paper is organized as follows: The general NMF algorithm is presented in Section 2 and the proposed denoising method is described in Section 3. An experiment using the TIMIT (Zue et al., 1990) speech corpus is presented in Section 4 and finally the performances are evaluated in terms of achieved signal enhancement in Section 5 before Section 6 concludes the paper.

2 Sparse Non-negative Matrix Factorization

2.1 NMF algorithm

NMF is a low-rank approximation technique for multivariate data decomposition. Given a real valued non-negative matrix **V** of size $n \times m$ and a positive integer $r < min(n, m)$, it aims to find a factorization of **V** into a $n \times r$ real matrix **W** and a $r \times m$ real matrix **H** such that:

$$\mathbf{V} \approx \mathbf{W} \cdot \mathbf{H} \quad (1)$$

The multivariate data to decompose is stacked into **V**, whose columns represent the different observations, and whose rows represent the different variables. In the case of information extraction from audio files, **V** could be the amplitude of the spectrogram and therefore, **W** would be a basis of spectral features when **H** would represent the levels of activation of each of those features along time. The rank r of the factorization corresponds to the number of elements present in the dictionary **W**, and thereof, to the number of rows within **H**.

NMF is an iterative process that can be fed with information about the contents to extract. As an illustration of this ability, an artificial spectrogram of a mixture of two chords, C and D, has been created. Figure 3 shows the initialization of the NMF algorithm. **V** is the spectrogram of the mixture in which the two chords contain only notes'fundamentals and overlap each other. The Algorithm is fed with the spectral content of the C chord.

Figure 4 shows that during the iterative process, the elements of **W** corresponding to the C chord remain unchanged while the other elements of **W** have been updated to fit the spectral content of the D chord. The output time activations within **H** correspond to the presence of both chords within the matrix **V**.

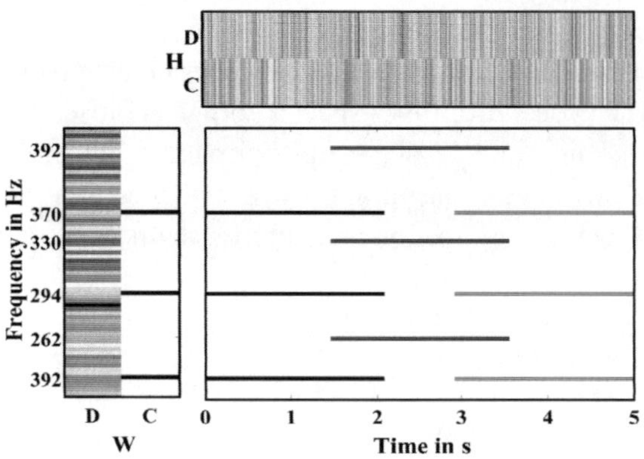

Figure 3: Illustration of the initialization of the NMF algorithm. The spectral content of the C chord is input into **W** while the other element of dictionary and activation coefficients in **H** are randomly initialized.

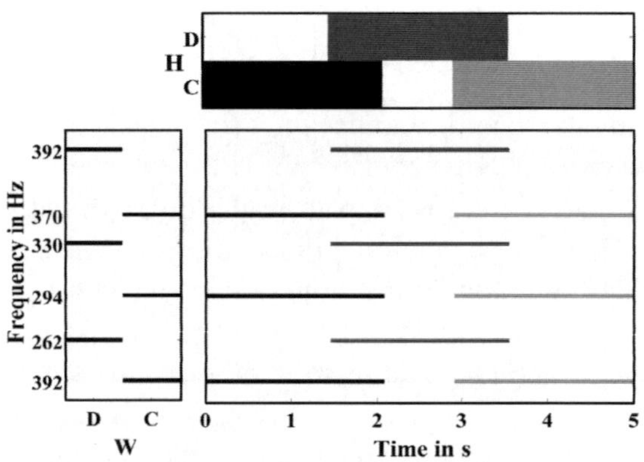

Figure 4: Illustration of the output of the NMF algorithm. The spectral content of the D chord has been learned while the updated **H** corresponds to the activations of the chords C and D along time.

2.2 Sparseness Constraint

The very definition of sparseness (or sparsity) is that a vector is sparse when most of its elements are zero. In its application to NMF, the addition of a sparseness constraint λ permits to trade off between the fitness of the factorization and the sparseness of **H**.

At each iteration, the process aims at reducing a cost function $\mathcal{C}$. In this paper, a generalized version of the Kullback Leibler divergence is used as cost function:

$$\mathcal{D}(\mathbf{V}, \mathbf{WH}) = \left\| \mathbf{V} \otimes \log \frac{\mathbf{V}}{\mathbf{W} \cdot \mathbf{H}} - \mathbf{V} + \mathbf{W} \cdot \mathbf{H} \right\| \quad (2)$$

In 2 the multiplication $\otimes$ and the division are element-wise. The sparseness constraint results in the new cost function:

$$\mathcal{C}(\mathbf{V}, \mathbf{WH}) = \mathcal{D}(\mathbf{V}, \mathbf{WH}) + \lambda \sum_{ij} \mathbf{H}_{ij} \quad (3)$$

The norm of each of the objects within **W** is fixed to unity.

3 Supervised NMF denoising

3.1 Method overview

The method is supervised in the sense that it uses a noise dictionary $\mathbf{W}_n$ built from a recording of the known noise to be reduced. The noise spectrogram Φ_n, *i.e.* the short-term fourier transform (STFT), is computed using a hamming window of 32ms and a 50% overlap. The magnitude $\mathbf{V}_n$ of Φ_n is input to the NMF algorithm with a sparseness constraint λ and an order r_n, providing the noise dictionary of r_n spectral vectors. The spectrogram $\mathbf{V}_s$ of the noisy speech is then input to the NMF algorithm along with $\mathbf{W}_n$ in order to obtain the denoised speech spectrogram.

3.2 Separation of the speech signal

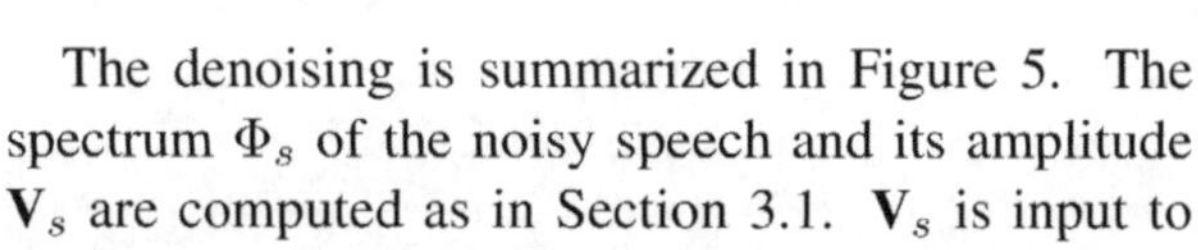

Figure 5: Overview of the NMF based denoising.

The denoising is summarized in Figure 5. The spectrum Φ_s of the noisy speech and its amplitude $\mathbf{V}_s$ are computed as in Section 3.1. $\mathbf{V}_s$ is input to the NMF algorithm along with $\mathbf{W}_n$. The order of factorization r is equal to $r_n + r_s$, r_s being the number of spectral vector used in the speech dictionary $\mathbf{W}_s$. Different sparseness constraint λ_n and λ_s can be applied to the activation matrices $\mathbf{H}_n$ and $\mathbf{H}_s$.

$$\begin{array}{lll} \text{Given} & \mathbf{V} \in \mathbb{R}_{+}^{n \times m}, r \in \mathbb{N}^* \; s.t. \; r < min(n,m) & \\ \text{minimize} & \mathcal{C}(\mathbf{V}, \mathbf{WH}) \; w.r.t. \; \mathbf{W}, \mathbf{H} & (4) \\ \text{subject to} & \mathbf{W} \in \mathbb{R}_{+}^{n \times r}, \; \mathbf{H} \in \mathbb{R}_{+}^{r \times m} & \end{array}$$

The update rules on **W** and **H** can be expressed as multiplicative updates:

$$\mathbf{W}_s \leftarrow \mathbf{W}_s \otimes \frac{\frac{\mathbf{V}}{\mathbf{W}_s \mathbf{H}_s} \cdot \mathbf{H}_s^T}{\mathbf{1} \cdot \mathbf{H}_s^T} \qquad \mathbf{H} \leftarrow \mathbf{H} \otimes \frac{\mathbf{W}^T \cdot \frac{\mathbf{V}}{\mathbf{WH}}}{\mathbf{W}^T \cdot \mathbf{1}} \qquad (5)$$

The NMF algorithm provides thereof $\mathbf{W}_s$ and $\mathbf{H}_s$ to be used to approximate the spectrogram of the denoised speech. Therefore, $\times$ being the matrix product:

$$\tilde{\mathbf{V}}_s = \mathbf{W}_s \times \mathbf{H}_s \qquad \tilde{\mathbf{V}}_n = \mathbf{W}_n \times \mathbf{H}_n$$
$$\tilde{\Phi}_s = \Phi_s \otimes \frac{\tilde{\mathbf{V}}_s}{\tilde{\mathbf{V}}_s + \tilde{\mathbf{V}}_n} \qquad (6)$$

The denoised speech signal is finally obtained by applying ISTFT on the spectrogram $\tilde{\mathbf{S}}_s$. The interested reader is referred to (O'Grady and Pearlmutter, 2006) for a more detailed discussion of the needed derivations for Eqs. (5)-(6).

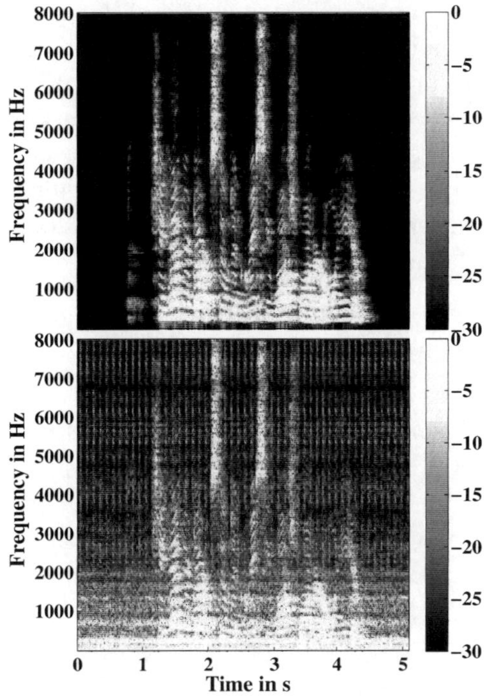

Figure 6: Spectrogram of a speech sentence from the TIMIT corpora: «*She had your dark suit in greasy wash water all year.*», clean (top) and with added sensors noise at SNR=10dB.

4 Experiment

4.1 Context

The robot platform Scitos A5 (Metralabs, 2012) can be used as a robotic assistant for elderly care. Its built-in microphones allow to interact with the robot using if their signal is analysed by an ASR system. However, while in motion, the robot uses ultrasonic sensors (c.f. Figure 2) to detect potential obstacles. Their constant activation and deactivation produces artifacts that can sever the ASR reliability. The following experiment aims to evaluate the efficiency of the denoising method proposed in Section 3 on speech signals corrupted by this specific sensors noise. The Figure 6 examplarily presents the spectrogram of a corrupted speech signal.

4.2 Protocol

The noise produced by the sensors and the room impulse response (RIR) have been recorded in a quiet office room using the robot's microphone. The test data has been built from the test portion of the TIMIT corpus (Zue et al., 1990). The clean speech files have been built concatenating a silent period of 0.5 seconds in their beginning, to allow for comparison with methods relying on a voice activity detector (VAD), and convolving it with the measured RIR. From those prepared clean files, noisy corpora have been built by adding the recorded sensors noise with a SNR set to 10, 5, 0 and -5 dB. In real scenarios, the SNR of the speech corrupted by the sensors noise vary between 5 and 10 dB depending on the loudness of the speaker and the distance between him and the robot.

When applying the NMF algorithm the cost function (3) has been used but no stop criterion has been set and a fixed number of 25 iterations has been run. $\mathbf{W}_n$ has been built by applying the NMF algorithm with $r_n = 64$ and $\lambda = 0$ to a 10 seconds noise recording. When applying the algorithm to the speech samples denoising, r has been set to 128. A different sparseness constraint has been applied to $\mathbf{H}_n$ and $\mathbf{H}_s$ with $\lambda_n = 0$ and $\lambda_s = 0.2$.

As a reference, the noisy sound samples have as

well been processed using a state-of-the-art single-channel noise reduction scheme, i.e. the decision-directed approach according to (Ephraim and Malah, 1985) based on two different noise estimation schemes, i.e. the minimum statistics approach (MS) as described in (Martin, 2001) and the minimum mean square error (MMSE) approach according to (Gerkmann and Hendriks, 2011).

5 Results

The achieved denoising is evaluated with the SNR of the denoised samples and with the noise reduction (NR) as described in (Loizou, 2007). For both scores, the presented values are the mean of the achieved scores on all tested speech samples and the standard deviation along the corpus. The results are presented in Figure 7 for varying input SNR and spectrograms of a denoised speech sample using the three methods is shown in Figure 8. It appears that the NMF based method provides better results, both in term of signal enhancement and of reliability.

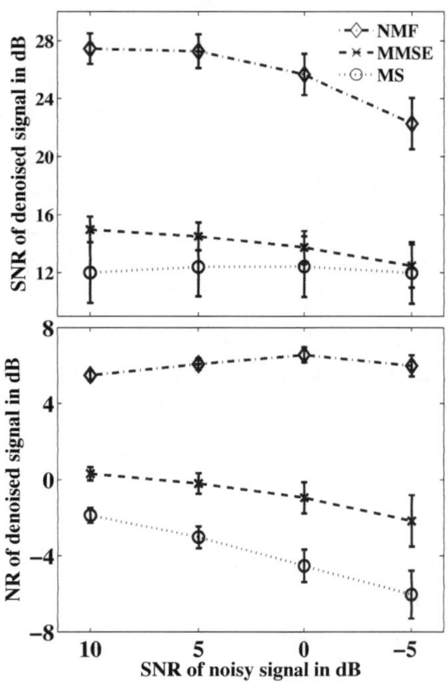

Figure 7: Mean and standard deviation of the achieved SNR and NR for the three tested methods and for different noise levels (SNR).

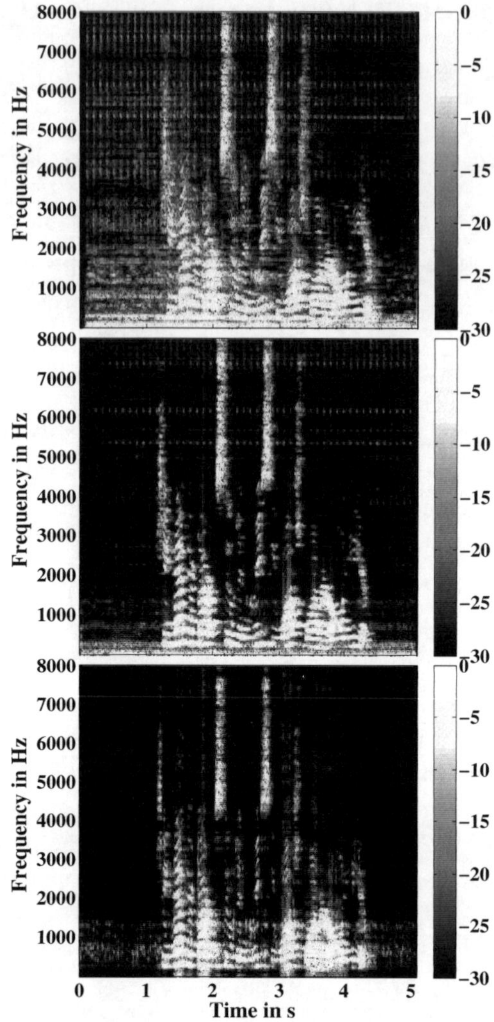

Figure 8: Spectrogram of a denoised signal using the three different methods, MS (top), MMSE (middle) and NMF.

6 Conclusion

A NMF based method to enhance speech signal when provided with spectral knowledge of the noise has been presented. This method has been applied to the reduction of the non stationary noise produced by the sensors of a robotic assistant. When tested on a corpus of speech signals, the proposed method achieved better performances than well known VAD based denoising.

Further works would include fine tuning of the method, such as determining the optimal number of iterations to obtain the best trade off between enhancement and computing cost, as well as the use of spectro temporal patches as elements of dictionary.

7 Acknowledgement

This work was partially supported by the "Adaptable Ambient Living Assistant" (ALIAS) project co-funded by the European Commission and the Federal Ministry of Education and Research (BMBF).

References

The European Ambient Assisted Living Innovation Alliance. 2009. *Ambient Assisted Living Roadmap.* VDI/VDE-IT AALIANCE Office.

G. Aragon-Camarasa, H. Fattah, and J. Paul Siebert. 2010. Towards a unified visual framework in a binocular active robot vision system. *Robotics and Autonomous Systems*, 58(3):276–286.

S. Boll, W. Heuten, E.M. Meyer, and M. , Meis. 2010. Development of a Multimodal Reminder System for Older Persons in their Residential Home. *Informatics for Health and Social Care, SI Ageing & Technology*, 35(4).

Selene Chew, Willie Tay, Danielle Smit, and Christoph Bartneck. 2010. Do social robots walk or roll? In Shuzhi Ge, Haizhou Li, John-John Cabibihan, and Yeow Tan, editors, *Social Robotics*, volume 6414 of *Lecture Notes in Computer Science*, pages 355–361. Springer Berlin / Heidelberg.

A. Cichocki, R. Zdunek, and S. Amari. New algorithms for non-negative matrix factorization in applications to blind source separation. In *Proc. of Acoustics, Speech and Signal Processing, 2006. ICASSP 2006.*, volume 5, pages V–V, Toulouse, France.

C.V. Cotton and D.P.W. Ellis. 2011. Spectral vs. spectro-temporal features for acoustic event detection. In *Proc. of 2011 IEEE Workshop on Applications of Signal Processing to Audio and Acoustics (WASPAA)*, pages 69 –72, New Paltz, NY, USA, oct.

Y. Ephraim and D. Malah. 1985. Speech enhancement using a minimum mean-square error log-spectral amplitude estimator. *IEEE Transactions on Acoustics, Speech and Signal Processing*, 33(2):443–445.

European Commision Staff. 2007. Working Document. Europes Demografic Future: Facts and Figures. Technical report, Commission of the European Communities.

T. Gerkmann and R.C. Hendriks. 2011. Noise power estimation based on the probability of speech presence. In *Proc. of 2011 IEEE Workshop on Applications of Signal Processing to Audio and Acoustics (WASPAA)*, pages 145–148, New Paltz, NY, USA.

S. Goetze, N. Moritz, J.E. Appell, M. Meis, C. Bartsch, and J. Bitzer. 2010. Acoustic user interfaces for ambient-assisted living technologies. *Informatics for Health and Social Care.*

S. Goetze, S. Fischer, N. Moritz, J.E. Appell, and F. Wallhoff. 2012. Multimodal human-machine interaction for service robots in home-care environments. Jeju, Republic of Korea.

X. Huang, A. Acero, H.W. Hon, et al. 2001. *Spoken language processing*, volume 15. Prentice Hall PTR New Jersey.

D.D. Lee and H.S. Seung. 2001. Algorithms for non-negative matrix factorization. *Advances in neural information processing systems*, 13.

C. Lisetti, F. Nasoz, C. LeRouge, O. Ozyer, and K. Alvarez. 2003. Developing multimodal intelligent affective interfaces for tele-home health care. *International Journal of Human-Computer Studies*, 59(1-2):245 – 255. Applications of Affective Computing in Human-Computer Interaction.

P.C. Loizou. 2007. *Speech Enhancement: Theory and Practice.* CRC Press Inc., Boca Raton, USA.

R. Martin. 2001. Noise power spectral density estimation based on optimal smoothing and minimum statistics. *IEEE Transactions on Speech and Audio Processing*, 9(5):504–512.

Metralabs. 2010. Technical manual.

Metralabs. 2012. http://www.metralabs.com.

P.D. O'Grady and B.A. Pearlmutter. 2006. Convolutive non-negative matrix factorisation with a sparseness constraint. In *Proc. of the 2006 16th IEEE Signal Processing Society Workshop on Machine Learning for Signal Processing*, Maynooth, Ireland.

B. Pfister and Kaufmann T. 2008. *Speech processing Fundamentals and mthods for speech synthesis and speech recognition (German original title: Sprachverarbeitun Grundlagen und Methoden der Sprachsynthese und Spracherkennung).* Springer, Berlin Heidelberg.

M.N. Schmidt, J. Larsen, and F.T. Hsiao. Wind noise reduction using non-negative sparse coding. In *Proc. of the 2007 17th IEEE Signal Processing Society Workshop on Machine Learning for Signal Processing*, Thessaloniki, Greece.

T. Virtanen. 2007. Monaural sound source separation by nonnegative matrix factorization with temporal continuity and sparseness criteria. *IEEE Transactions on Audio, Speech, and Language Processing*, 15(3):1066–1074.

M. Wölfel, J.W. McDonough, and Inc Ebrary. 2009. *Distant speech recognition.* Wiley Online Library.

K. Youssef, S. Argentieri, and J.L. Zarader. Binaural speaker recognition for humanoid robots. In *Proc. of 2010 11th International Conference on Control Automation Robotics & Vision (ICARCV)*, Singapore, Republic of Singapore.

V. Zue, S. Seneff, and J. Glass. 1990. Speech database development at MIT: TIMIT and beyond. *Speech Communication*, 9(4):351–356.

Towards a Self-Learning Assistive Vocal Interface: Vocabulary and Grammar Learning

Janneke van de Loo[1], Jort F. Gemmeke[2], Guy De Pauw[1]
Joris Driesen[2], Hugo Van hamme[2], Walter Daelemans[1]
[1]CLiPS - Computational Linguistics, University of Antwerp, Antwerp, Belgium
[2]ESAT - PSI Speech Group, KU Leuven, Leuven, Belgium
janneke.vandeloo@ua.ac.be, jort.gemmeke@esat.kuleuven.be, guy.depauw@ua.ac.be, joris.driesen@esat.kuleuven.be, hugo.vanhamme@esat.kuleuven.be, walter.daelemans@ua.ac.be

Abstract

This paper introduces research within the ALADIN project, which aims to develop an assistive vocal interface for people with a physical impairment. In contrast to existing approaches, the vocal interface is self-learning, which means it can be used with any language, dialect, vocabulary and grammar. This paper describes the overall learning framework, and the two components that will provide vocabulary learning and grammar induction. In addition, the paper describes encouraging results of early implementations of these vocabulary and grammar learning components, applied to recorded sessions of a vocally guided card game, Patience.

1 Introduction

Voice control of devices we use in our daily lives is still perceived as a luxury, since often cheaper and more straightforward alternatives are available, such as pushing a button or using remote controls. But what if pushing buttons is not trivial? Physically impaired people with restricted (upper) limb motor control are permanently in the situation where voice control could significantly simplify some of the tasks they want to perform (Noyes and Frankish, 1992). By regaining the ability to control more devices in the living environment, voice control could contribute to their independence of living and their quality of life.

Unfortunately, the speech recognition technology employed for voice control still lacks robustness to speaking style, regional accents and noise, so that users are typically forced to adhere to a restrictive grammar and vocabulary in order to successfully *command and control* a device.

In this paper we describe research in the ALADIN project[1], which aims to develop an assistive vocal interface for people with a physical impairment. In contrast to existing vocal interfaces, the vocal interface is self-learning: The interface should automatically **learn** what the user means with commands, which words are used and what the user's vocal characteristics are. Users should formulate commands as they like, using the words and grammatical constructs they like and only addressing the functionality they are interested in.

We distinguish two separate modules that establish self-learning: The **word finding** module works on the acoustic level and attempts to automatically induce the vocabulary of the user during training, by associating recurring acoustic patterns (commands) with observed changes in the user's environment (control). The **grammar induction** module works alongside the word finding module to automatically detect the compositionality of the user's utterances, further enabling the user to freely express commands in their own words.

This paper presents a functional description of the ALADIN learning framework and describes feasibility experiments with the word finding and grammar induction modules. In Section 2 we outline the overall learning framework, the knowledge representation that is used and the rationale behind the word finding and grammar induction modules. In Section 3 we briefly describe the *Patience* corpus used

[1]Adaptation and Learning for Assistive Domestic Vocal INterfaces. Project page: http://www.esat.kuleuven.be/psi/spraak/projects/ALADIN

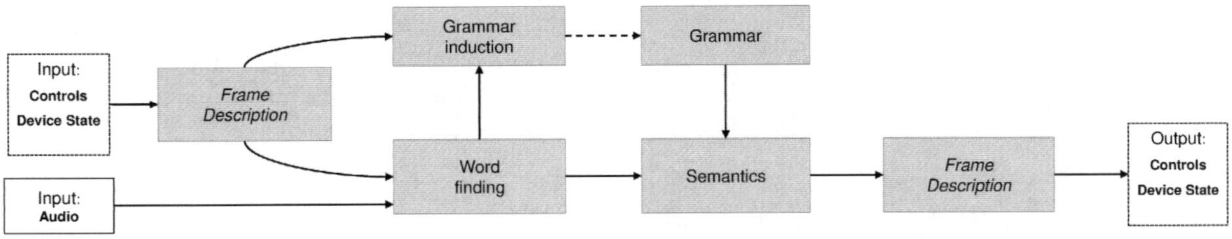

Figure 1: Schematic overview of the ALADIN framework.

in the feasibility experiments, as well as the experimental setup. In Section 4 we show and discuss our experimental results and we present our conclusions and thoughts on future work in Section 5.

2 The ALADIN framework

The ALADIN learning framework consists of several modules, which are shown schematically in Fig. 1. On the left-hand side, the provided input is shown, which consists of a spoken utterance (command) coupled with a control input, such as the button press on a remote control or a mouse click, possibly augmented with the internal state of a device (for example the current volume of a television).

In order to provide a common framework for all possible actions we wish to distinguish, we adopt the use of *frames*, a data structure that encapsulates the control inputs and/or device states relevant to the execution of each action. Frames consist of one or multiple slots, which each can take a single value from a set of predefined values. In Section 2.1 we discuss the frame representation in detail.

During training, the *word finding* module builds acoustic representations of recurring acoustic patterns, given a (small) set of training commands, each described by a frame description and features extracted from the audio signal. Using the frame description, the module maps such acoustic representations to each slot-value pair in each frame. When using the framework for decoding spoken commands, the output of the module is a score for each slot-value pair in each frame, representing the probability that this slot-value pair was present in the spoken command.

During training, the *grammar induction* module builds a model of the grammatical constructs employed by the user, using the frame description and the output of the word finding module. The output of the word finding module consists of estimates of the slot-value pair scores described above, based on the presence of automatically derived recurring acoustic patterns.

The *semantics* module, operational during decoding, processes the output of the word finding module to create a single frame description most likely to match the spoken command. This can then be converted to a control representation the target device can work with. The module can make use of a *grammar* module that describes which slot-value pair combinations (and sequences) are likely to occur for each frame. Such a grammar description should ideally be provided by the grammar induction module, but could optionally be hand-crafted.

2.1 Frame description

Each action that can be performed with a device is represented in the form of a *frame*. A frame is a data structure that represents the semantic concepts that are relevant to the execution of the action and which users of the command and control (henceforth C&C) application are likely to refer to in their commands. It usually contains one or multiple slots, each associated with a single value. The slots in an action frame represent relevant properties of the action. Such frame-based semantic representations have previously been successfully deployed in C&C applications and spoken dialog systems (Wang et al., 2005).

For our research, we distinguish three types of frames. The first, the *action frame*, is automatically generated during training by the device that is controlled with a conventional control method, such as button presses. Depending on the frame, more slots may be defined than are likely to be referred to in any single command. The second frame type, the *oracle*

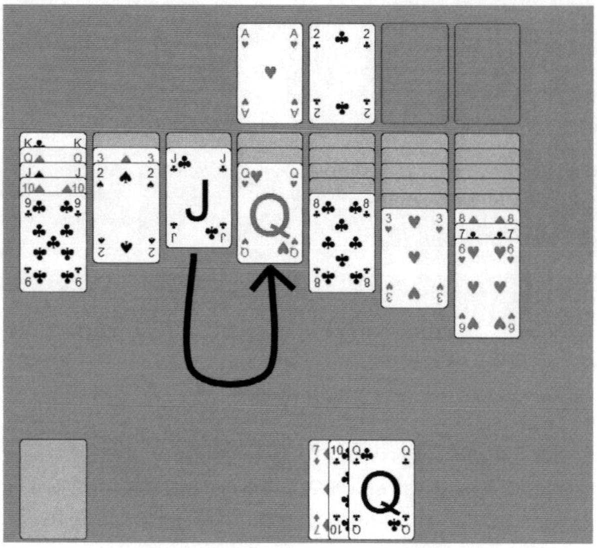

Frame Slot	Value
<from_suit>	c
<from_value>	11
<from_column>	3
<from_hand>	-
<to_suit>	h
<to_value>	12
<to_foundation>	-
<to_column>	4

Figure 2: An example of a Patience move and the automatically generated `movecard` action frame. A card is defined as the combination of a `suit` - (h)earts, (d)iamonds, (c)lubs or (s)pades - and a `value`, from ace (1) to king (13). We also distinguish slots for the 'hand' at the bottom, the seven columns in the center of the playing field and the four foundation stacks at the top right.

action frame, is a manually constructed subset of the action frame based on a transcription of the spoken command. In this subset, only those slots that are referred to in the spoken command, are filled in. Finally, we define the *oracle command frame*, which is a version of the oracle action frame that can assign multiple values to each slot in order to deal with possible ambiguities in the spoken command.

We will illustrate these frame types with an example from one the target applications in the ALADIN project: a voice-controlled version of the card game *Patience*. In this game, one of the possible actions is moving a card in the playing field. This action is described by an action frame dubbed `movecard`, which contains slots specifying which card is moved and to which position it is moved. Fig. 2 shows an example of such a move, and the automatically generated action frame description of that move.

For instance, if the move in Fig. 2 was associated with the spoken command *"put the jack of clubs on the red queen"*, the oracle action frame of that particular move would only have the following slot values filled in: <from_suit>=c, <from_value>=11, <to_suit>=h and <to_value>=12, since the columns are not referred to in the spoken command. Also, since no slot was defined that is associated with the *color* of the card, the spoken command is ambiguous and during decoding, such a command might also be associated with a frame containing the slot-value pair <to_suit>=d. As a result, the oracle command frame will be constructed with <to_suit>=h,d rather than <to_suit>=h.

2.2 Word finding

The word finding module is tasked with creating acoustic representations of recurring acoustic patterns, guided by action frames. As such, the learning task is only weakly supervised: rather than having knowledge of the sequence of words that were spoken, as common in Automatic Speech Recognition (ASR), we only have knowledge of the slot-value pairs in the action frame, each of which may have been referred to in the utterance with one or multiple words, and in any order. To meet these requirements, we turn to a technique called non-negative matrix factorization (NMF).

2.2.1 Supervised NMF

NMF is an algorithm that factorizes a non-negative $M \times N$ matrix $\mathbf{V}$ into a non-negative $M \times R$ matrix $\mathbf{W}$ and a non-negative $R \times N$ matrix $\mathbf{H}$: $\mathbf{V} \approx \mathbf{W} \cdot \mathbf{H}$. In our approach, we construct the NMF problem as follows:

$$\mathbf{V} = \begin{bmatrix} \mathbf{V_0} \\ \mathbf{V_1} \end{bmatrix} \approx \begin{bmatrix} \mathbf{W_0} \\ \mathbf{W_1} \end{bmatrix} \mathbf{H} = \mathbf{WH} \qquad (1)$$

with the matrix $\mathbf{V_1}$ composed of N spoken commands, each represented by a vectorial representation of dimension M_1. The columns of $\mathbf{V_0}$ associate each spoken command with a label vector of dimension M_0 that represents the frequency with which a particular label occurred in that spoken command. After factorization, the matrix $\mathbf{W_1}$ contains R acoustic patterns of dimension M_1, and the matrix $\mathbf{H}$ indicates the weights with which these R acoustic patterns are linearly combined for each spoken command n, $1 \leq n \leq N$, to form the observed spoken commands in $\mathbf{V_1}$. The columns of the matrix $\mathbf{W_0}$ describe the mapping between the R acoustic patterns in $\mathbf{W_1}$ and the M_0 labels that can be associated with each spoken command. In addition to columns of $\mathbf{W_1}$ associated with labels, we use a number of so-called 'garbage columns' to capture acoustic representations not associated with labels, for example to capture less meaningful words such as 'please'.

To decode a spoken command (the 'testing' phase), we find a vector $\mathbf{h}$ for which holds: $\mathbf{v_1}^{tst} = \mathbf{W_1}\mathbf{h}^{tst}$, with $\mathbf{W_1}$ the matrix found during training. $\mathbf{v}_1^{tst}$ is the M_1 dimensional acoustic representation of the spoken command we wish to decode, and $\mathbf{h}^{tst}$ is the R-dimensional vector that indicates which acoustic patterns in $\mathbf{W_1}$ need to be linearly combined to explain $\mathbf{v}_1^{tst}$. Finally, we calculate the label association with the spoken command $\mathbf{v}_1^{tst}$ using: $\mathbf{a} = \mathbf{W_0}\mathbf{h}^{tst}$, where $\mathbf{a}$ is a M_0 dimensional vector giving a score for each label.

For more details on how to carry out these factorizations, we refer the reader to Lee and Seung (1999). For a discussion on representing spoken commands of varying length as a M_1-dimensional vector, and the constraints under which it holds that the spoken command is the linear combination of R such vectors from $\mathbf{W_1}$, we refer the reader to (Van hamme, 2008; Driesen and Van hamme, 2012; Driesen et al., 2012) and the references therein.

2.2.2 Frame decoding

In our framework, we consider each unique slot-value pair of each frame (for example <to_suit>=h of the frame movecard) as a single label, making the total number of labels M_0 equal to the cumulative number of different values in all slots in all frames. This way, each frame description is uniquely mapped to a binary vector $\mathbf{v_1}$, and likewise, the decoded label vector $\mathbf{a}$ is uniquely mapped back to a frame description.

Put	*the*	*jack*	*of*	*clubs*	*on*	*the*	*queen*	*of*	*hearts*
O	O	I_FV	O	I_FS	O	O	I_TV	O	I_TS

Figure 3: Example of a command transcription, annotated with concept tags.

2.3 Grammar induction

The task of the grammar module is to automatically induce a grammar during the training phase, that detects the compositionality of the utterances and relates it to the associated meaning. In this case, the grammatical properties of the utterances are associated with action frames, containing slots and values. This grammar induction is performed on the basis of the output of the word finding module (hypothesized 'word' units, represented as acoustic patterns and possibly associated frame slot values) and the generated frame descriptions of the actions. Furthermore, the grammar may also serve as an additional aid during the decoding process, by providing information regarding the probability of specific frame slot sequences in the data.

There are different options with respect to the type of grammar that can be induced. It could for instance be a traditional context-free grammar, meaning that the contents of the frame description of the action are derived on the basis of a parse tree of the utterance. Unfortunately, context-free grammars have been proven to be very hard to automatically induce (de Marcken, 1999; Klein, 2005), particularly on the basis of limited training data.

Encouraging results have been reported in the unsupervised induction of sequence tags (Collobert et al., 2011). In the context of the ALADIN project, we therefore decided to adopt a *concept tagging* approach as a *shallow grammar* interface between utterance and meaning. In this vein, each command is segmented into chunks of words, which are tagged with the semantic concepts (i.e. frame slots) to which they refer.

We use a tagging framework which is based on so-called `IOB` tagging, commonly used in the context of phrase chunking tasks (Ramshaw and Marcus, 1995). Words inside a chunk are labeled with a tag starting with `I` and words outside the chunks are labeled with an `O` tag, which means that they do not refer to any concept in the action frame. Fig. 3 illustrates the concept tagging approach for an example command.

3 Experimental setup

The experiments described in this paper pertain to a vocal interface for the card game Patience. This presents an appropriate case study, since a C&C interface for this game needs to learn a non-trivial, but fairly restrictive vocabulary and grammar. Commands such as "*put the four of clubs on the five of hearts*" or "*put the three of hearts in column four*" are not replaceable by holistic commands, and identifying the individual components of the utterance and their interrelation is essential for the derivation of its meaning. This makes the Patience game a more interesting test case than domotica applications such as controlling lights, doors or a television, where the collection of unordered sets of keywords is usually sufficient to understand the commands.

In this section, we will describe the corpus collected to enable this case study, as well as the setup for exploratory experiments with the techniques outlined in Section 2.

3.1 Patience corpus

The Patience corpus consists of more than two thousand spoken commands in (Belgian) Dutch[2], transcribed and manually annotated with *concept tags*. Eight participants were asked to play Patience on a computer using spoken commands, which were subsequently executed by the experimenter. The participants were told to advance the game by using their own commands freely, in terms of vocabulary and grammatical constructs. The audio signals of the commands were recorded and the associated actions were stored in the form of action frames. There are two types of frames: a `movecard` frame, describing the movement of a card on the playing field (e.g. Fig. 2), and a `dealcard` frame that contains no frame slots, but simply triggers a new hand. Oracle action and command frames were derived on the basis of the automatically generated action frames and the manually annotated concept tags.

Each participant played in two separate sessions, with at least three weeks in between, so as to capture potential variation in command use over time. The participants' ages range between 22 and 73 and we balanced for gender and education level. We collected between 223 and 278 commands (in four to six games) per participant. The total number of collected commands is 2020, which means an average of 253 commands per participant and the average number of moves per game is 55. The total number of frame slot-value pairs is 63.

The experimental setup tries to mimic the ALADIN learning situation as much as possible. For each participant, a separate learning curve was made, since the learning process in the targeted ALADIN application will be personalized as well. For each learning curve, the last fifty utterances of a participant were used as a constant test set. The remaining utterances of the same participant were used as training material. The chronological order of the commands, as they were uttered by the participant, was preserved, in order to account for the development of the users' command structure and vocabulary use during the games. In each experiment, the first *k* utterances were used as training data, *k* being an increasing number of slices of ten utterances for the grammar induction experiments and 25 utterances for the word finding experiments.

3.2 Word finding

Spoken commands are represented by a Histogram of Acoustic Co-occurrence (HAC) features (Van hamme, 2008), constructed as follows: First, we extract mel-cepstral coefficients (MFCC) from audio signals sampled at 16kHz, framed using time windows of 25ms and shifted in increments of 10ms. From each of these frames, 13 cepstral coefficients, along with their first and second order differences are determined, yielding a 39 dimensional feature vector. Mean and variance normalization are applied on a per-utterance basis. Second, k-means clustering of 50000 randomly selected frames is used to create a Vector Quantization codebook with 200 codewords for each speaker, using k-means clustering. Finally, three sets of HAC features are constructed by counting the co-occurrences of the audio expressed as VQ codewords, with time lags of 2, 5 and 9 frames. The final feature dimension M_1 is thus $M_1 = 3 \times 200^2 = 120000$.

In these initial experiments, we use the oracle action frames to provide supervision. In the NMF learning framework, two acoustic representations were assigned to each label, with an additional 15 representations used as garbage columns. The total number of acoustic representations R is thus

[2] Note however that the ALADIN system is inherently language independent, which is why we present the examples in English.

$R = 2 \times 63 + 15 = 141$. For training, $\mathbf{W_1}$ is initialized randomly and $\mathbf{W_0}$ is initialized so that two columns are mainly associated with each label (i.e., a one in the corresponding label position and a small $([0, 1e-5])$ random value for the other labels). The remaining 15 garbage columns are randomly initialized. Finally, the entries of $\mathbf{V_1}$ and $\mathbf{V_0}$ are scaled so their cumulative weight is equal. During training, the rows of $\mathbf{H}$ pertaining to non-garbage columns in $\mathbf{W_0}$ are initialized to be the same as $\mathbf{V_0}$, with a small $([0, 1e-5])$ random value replacing values that are zero. The rows of $\mathbf{H}$ pertaining to garbage columns are initialized randomly. For the NMF factorization, we minimized the Kullback-Leibler divergence using 100 iterations of the procedure described in Lee and Seung (1999).

In these experiments, frame decoding is guided by a hand-crafted grammar, rather than an automatically induced grammar. We defined 38 grammar rules corresponding to various possible slot sequences, under the assumption that `from` slots precede `to` slots, and that `_suit` slots precede `_value slots`. These 38 rules also include various slot sequences in which the command was underspecified. A pilot experiment showed that this grammar covers 98% to 100% of the spoken commands, depending on the speaker. The hand-crafted grammar was implemented as a labelvector-to-labelvector bigram transition matrix, and Viterbi decoding was used to generate a possible frame description for each grammar rule. For scoring, the most likely frame description was selected based on the most likely Viterbi path across grammar rules. Finally, we express results in terms of *slot-value accuracy*, which is the ratio of the number of slot-value pairs correctly selected, according to the oracle command frame, and the total number of slot-value pairs in the oracle command frame (expressed as a percentage).

3.3 Grammar induction

The exploratory experiments for the grammar induction module serve as a proof-of-the-principle experiment that showcases the *learnability* of the task in optimal conditions and focuses on the minimally required amount of training data needed to bootstrap successful concept tagging. In these supervised learning experiments, the annotated corpus is used as training material for a data-driven tagger, which is subsequently used to tag previously unseen data. As our tagger of choice, we opted for MBT, the memory-based tagger (Daelemans et al., 2010), although any type of data-driven tagger can be used.

In the targeted ALADIN application, the number of utterances used to train the system should be as small as possible, i.e. the training phase should be as brief as possible in order to limit the amount of extraneous physical work or assistance needed for training by the physically impaired person. In order to get an idea of the minimal number of training utterances needed to enable successful concept tagging, we evaluated the supervised tagging performance with increasing amounts of training data, resulting in learning curves.

The metric used for the evaluation of the concept tagger is the micro-averaged F-score of the predicted `I` chunks: the harmonic mean of the precision and recall of the chunks with `I` labels (i.e. referring to slots in de frame description). This means that the concept tags as well as the boundaries of the predicted chunks are included in the evaluation. Feature selection was performed on the basis of a development set (last 25% of the training data) and establishes the best combination of disambiguation features, such as the number of (disambiguated) concept tags to the left, the tokens themselves (left/right/focus) and ambiguous tags (focus token and right context). We compare our results against a baseline condition, in which only the focus word is used as a feature, in order to see the relative effect of the use of context information by the tagger.

4 Results and discussion

4.1 Word finding

In Fig. 4a we can observe the results obtained with a learning framework that combines word finding with hand-crafted grammars. From these results, we can observe that the slot-value accuracy obtained after using all available training material, varies between 40.4% for speaker 4 and 76.0% for speaker 1. We can also observe that overall, the results for all speakers show a fairly linear increase in accuracy as more training material becomes available. The fact that we do not yet observe that the accuracy levels off with increasing training data, indicates that the results are likely to further improve with more training data.

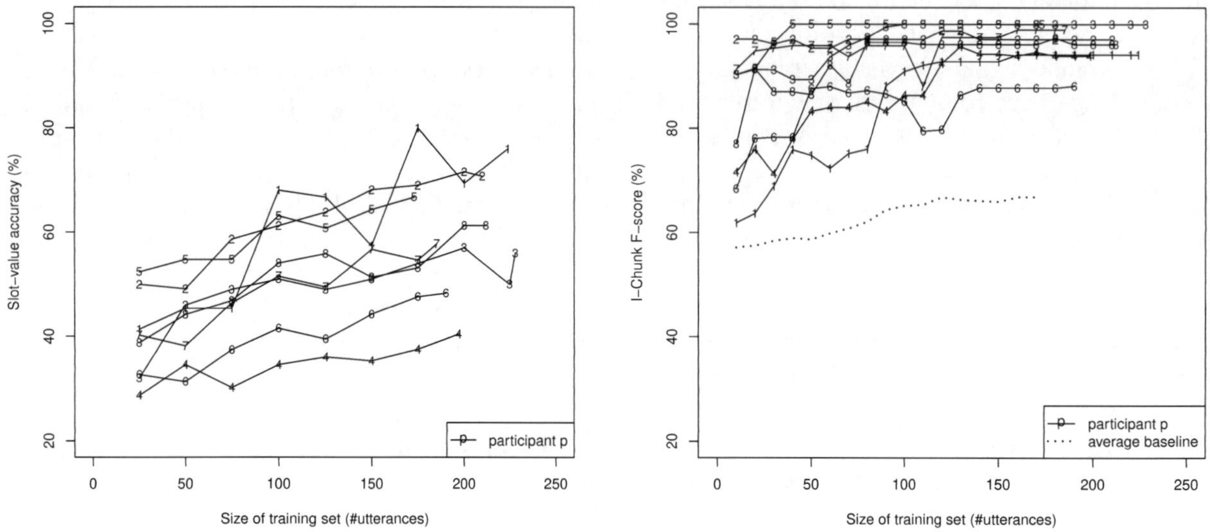

(a) Word finding results

(b) Grammar induction results

Figure 4: Learning curves viz. word finding accuracy (left) and grammar induction I chunk F-score (right).

This is also likely given the complexity of the learning task: In Patience, about half of the spoken commands pertains to `dealcard` frames, which means it is very likely that some slot-value pairs have never even occurred in the training data, even after 200 spoken commands. We expect, however, that we need at least a few repetitions of each slot-value pair to build a robust acoustic representation: the accuracy of correctly detecting the `dealcard` frame, which has many repetitions in the training data, is close to 100% for all speakers. Given such data scarcity, the fact that we obtain accuracies up to 76% is encouraging.

Another observation that can be made is that for some speakers, such as speaker 1, there is a larger variation between consecutive training sizes - for example for speaker 1 the best accuracy is obtained for a training size of 175 spoken commands. There are several possible reasons. For one, even though the NMF learning problem is initialized using the constraints imposed by the frame labeling, the factorization process may not achieve the global optimal solution during training. This could be addressed by performing multiple experiments with different random initializations (Driesen et al., 2012).

Another issue is that the number of `dealcard` frames varies between speakers, due to the relatively small test set size of fifty spoken utterances. With the `dealcard` typically recognized correctly, this may account both for some of the differences between speakers, as well as for the variation between training sizes observed for some speakers: If the number of `movecard` frames in the test set is small, this makes the average accuracy more sensitive to errors on these frames. This issue could be addressed by an alternative evaluation scheme in which multiple occurrences of the same utterance are only counted once.

4.2 Grammar induction

Fig. 4b displays the learning curves for the supervised concept tagging experiments. There is a large amount of variation between the participants in accuracy using the first 100 training utterances. Six out of eight curves reach 95% or more with 130 training utterances, and level off after that. For two participants, the accuracies reach 100%, with training set sizes of 40 and 100 utterances respectively. The baseline accuracies, averaged across all participants, are also shown in Fig. 4b. These are significantly superseded by the individual learning curves with optimized features, showing that the use of context information is important to enable successful concept tagging on this dataset.

The fact that the tag accuracy for participant 6 remains relatively low (around 88%) is mainly due to a rather high level of inconsistency and ambiguity in the command structures that were used. One remarkable source of errors in this case is a structure repeatedly occurring in the test set and occurring only twice in the largest training set. It is a particularly difficult one: a structure in which multiple cards are specified to be moved (in one pile), such as in "*the black three, the red four and the black five to the red six*". In such cases, only the highest card of the moved pile (*black five* in the example) should be labeled with `I_FS` and `I_FV` tags (since only that card is represented in the action frame) and the lower cards should be tagged with `O` tags.

The commands given by participants 2 and 5 were structurally very consistent throughout the games, resulting in very fast learning. Participant 5's learning curve reaches a tag accuracy of 100% using as little as forty training utterances, underlining the learnability of this task in optimal conditions. Participant 3's curve reaches 100% accuracy, but has a dip at the beginning of the curve. This is due to the fact that in the utterance numbers 20-50, the suit specification was often dropped (e.g. "*the three on the four*"), whereas in the utterances before and after that, the suit specification was often included.

5 Conclusions and future work

In this paper, we introduced a self-learning framework for a vocal interface that can be used with any language, dialect, vocabulary and grammar. In addition to a description of the overall learning framework and its internal knowledge representation, we described the two building blocks that will provide vocabulary learning and grammar induction. Our experiments show encouraging results, both for vocabulary learning and grammar induction, when applied to the very challenging task of a vocally guided card game, Patience, with only limited training data.

Although the word finding experiments use the oracle action frames rather than the automatically generated frames as supervision information, the preliminary experiments shown in this work are promising enough to have confidence that even with this additional source of uncertainty, the goal of a self-learning vocal interface is feasible. The concept tagging experiments show that this type of representation is learnable in a supervised way with a high degree of accuracy on the basis of a relatively limited amount of data.

Future experiments will investigate how unsupervised learning techniques can be used to bootstrap concept tagging without using annotated and manually transcribed data. This will enable the output of the grammar module to replace the manually crafted grammar currently used by the word finding module. Since the learning curves for the word finding module still show significant room for improvement, more data will need to be collected to adequately investigate the interaction between the two modules.

We expect the word finding results to improve once speaker-specific grammars, provided by the grammar induction module, can be incorporated. The hand-crafted grammar employed in the word finding experiments include almost all variations, while a speaker-specific grammar will typically be more restrictive. Another practical approach to improve the user experience is to have the ALADIN system produce an ordered set of several possible frame descriptions, based on the knowledge of the playing field and the rules of the game. Preliminary experiments revealed that even with a small ordered set of only five frame candidates, the slot-value accuracy of the Patience word finding experiments increased by 10% to 20% absolute. Furthermore, we expect the number of repetitions needed for each slot-value pair to reduce substantially if we allow *sharing* of the acoustic representations between slots. For example, it is very likely that the user will refer to the suit of 'hearts' the same way, regardless of whether it occurs in a `from` slot or in a `to` slot.

While the self-learning modules have not yet been integrated and while there is still ample room for improvement within each module individually, the results of the feasibility experiments described in this paper are encouraging. The insights gained from these experiments form a solid basis for further experimentation and will serve to further streamline the development of a language independent, self-learning command & control vocal interface for people with a physical impairment.

Acknowledgments

This research was funded by IWT-SBO grant 100049 (ALADIN).

References

R. Collobert, J. Weston, L. Bottou, M. Karlen, K. Kavukcuoglu, and P. Kuksa. 2011. Natural language processing (almost) from scratch. *Journal of Machine Learning Research*, 12:2461–2505.

W. Daelemans, J. Zavrel, A. van den Bosch, and K. Van der Sloot. 2010. MBT: Memory-based tagger, version 3.2, reference guide. Technical Report 10-04, University of Tilburg.

C. de Marcken. 1999. On the unsupervised induction of phrase-structure grammars. In S. Armstrong, K. Church, P. Isabelle, S. Manzi, E. Tzoukermann, and D. Yarowsky, editors, *Natural Language Processing Using Very Large Corpora*, volume 11 of *Text, Speech and Language Technology*, pages 191–208. Kluwer Academic Publishers.

J. Driesen and H. Van hamme. 2012. Fast word acquisition in an NMF-based learning framework. In *Proceedings of the 36th International Conference on Acoustics, Speech and Signal Processing*, Kyoto, Japan.

J. Driesen, J.F. Gemmeke, and H. Van hamme. 2012. Weakly supervised keyword learning using sparse representations of speech. In *Proceedings of the 36th International Conference on Acoustics, Speech and Signal Processing*, Kyoto, Japan.

D. Klein. 2005. *The Unsupervised Learning of Natural Language Structure*. Ph.D. thesis, Stanford University.

D.D. Lee and H.S. Seung. 1999. Learning the parts of objects by nonnegative matrix factorization. *Nature*, 401:788–791.

J. Noyes and C. Frankish. 1992. Speech recognition technology for individuals with disabilities. *Augmentative and Alternative Communication*, 8(4):297–303.

L.A. Ramshaw and M.P. Marcus. 1995. Text chunking using transformation-based learning. In *Proceedings of the Third ACL Workshop on Very Large Corpora*, pages 82–94, Cambridge, USA.

H. Van hamme. 2008. Hac-models: a novel approach to continuous speech recognition. In *Proceedings International Conference on Spoken Language Processing*, pages 2554–2557, Brisbane, Australia.

Y. Wang, L. Deng, and A. Acero. 2005. An introduction to statistical spoken language understanding. *IEEE Signal Processing Magazine*, 22(5):16–31.

A Bengali Speech Synthesizer on Android OS

Sankar Mukherjee, Shyamal Kumar Das Mandal
Center for Educational Technology
Indian Institute of Technology Kharagpur
sankar1535@gmail.com
sdasmandal@cet.iitkgp.ernet.in

Abstract

Different Bengali TTS systems are already available on a resourceful platform such as a personal computer. However, porting these systems to a resource limited device such as a mobile phone is not an easy task. Practical aspects including application size and processing time have to be concerned. This paper describes the implementation of a Bengali speech synthesizer on a mobile device. For speech generation we used Epoch Synchronous Non Overlap Add (ESNOLA) based concatenative speech synthesis technique which uses the partnemes as the smallest signal units for concatenations.

1 Introduction

Technologies for handheld devices with open platforms have made rapid progresses. Recently open-platforms Android is getting momentum. Mobile devices with microphone and speaker, video camera, touch screen, GPS, etc, are served as sensors for experiencing with augmented reality in human life. Speech synthesis may become one of the main modalities on mobile devices as the screen size and several application scenarios (e.g., driving, jogging) limits the use of visual modality. Optimizing a speech synthesis system on mobile devices is a challenging task because the storage capacity and the computing performance are limited. Even if the storage capacity of the device is quite high, it is unlikely that users will let e.g., the half of their storage for speech synthesis purposes. So it is necessary to have small footprint.

Until now, text-to-speech applications have been developed on many platforms, such as PC, electronic dictionary and mobile device. However, most applications are for English language. Early works on developing a TTS system on a mobile device focused mainly on migration of an existing TTS system from a resourceful platform to a resource-limited platform (W. Black and K. A. Lenzo, 2001; Hoffmann, R et al., 2003). Most of the effort was spent on code optimization and database compression. Since the space was quite limited, only a small diphone database could be utilized which reduced the quality of synthesized speech. To improve the output speech quality some researchers attempted to apply a unit selection technique on a resource limited device. (Tsiakoulis, et al, 2008) used a database small enough for an embedded device without much reduction in speech quality. (Pucher, M. and Frohlich, 2005) used a large unit selection database but synthesize an output speech on a server and then transferred the wave form to a mobile device over a network.

Bengali TTS systems have been already developed and produced reasonably acceptable synthesized output quality on PC, as Shyamal Kumar Das Mandal and Asoke Kumar Datta (2007). However the same has not yet been implemented for resource-limited or embedded devices such as mobile phones.

The goal of our research is to develop a Bengali speech synthesizer that can produce an acceptable quality of synthesized output in almost real-time on mobile device.

2 Speech Synthesis Techniques

Speech synthesis involves the algorithmic conversion of input text data to speech waveforms. Speech synthesizers are characterized by the methods used for storage, encoding and synthesis of the speech. The synthesis method is determined by the vocabulary size, as all possible utterances of the language need to be modeled. There are different approaches to speech synthesis, such as rule-based, articulatory modeling and concatenative technique. Recent speech research has been directed towards concatenative speech synthesizers. We develop our synthesizer based on Epoch Synchronous Non Overlap Add (ESNOLA) concatenative speech synthesis method, as Shyamal Kumar Das Mandal and Asoke Kumar Datta (2007).

ESNOLA allows judicious selection of signal segment so that the smaller fundamental parts of the phoneme may be used as unit for reducing both the number and the size of the signal elements in the dictionary. This is called Partnemes. Further the methodology of concatenation provides adequate processing for proper matching between different segments during concatenation and it supports unlimited vocabulary without decreasing the quality.

3 TTS System Based on ESNOLA Method

A schematic diagram of the speech synthesis system is shown in Figure 1.

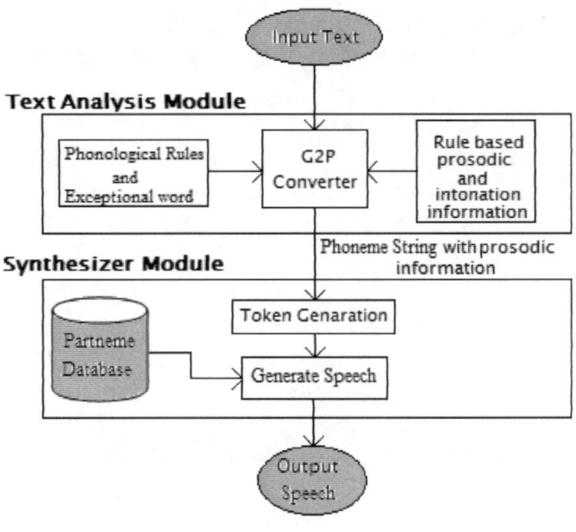

Figure 1: Text-to-Speech process diagram

The Text-to-Speech system consists of two main parts: Text analysis module and Synthesizer module.

3.1 Text Analysis Module

The text analysis module has two broad sections one is the phonological analysis module and other is the analysis of the text for prosody and intonation. Bangla is a syllabic script, phonological analysis i.e. Grapheme to Phoneme conversation is a formidable problem (Suniti Kumar Chatterji, 2002; Sarkar Pabitra, 1990) specially found in case of two vowels /a/ and /e/ and some consonant clusters. A set of phonological rule including exception dictionary is developed and implemented, as (Basu, J et al., 2009). The phonological rules also depend upon POS and semantics. But due to its requirement of language analysis it is taken care by exception dictionary.

3.2 Synthesizer Module

Synthesizer module has two parts. First generate token and second combine splices of pre-recorded speech and generate the synthesized voice output using ESNOLA approach as in Shyamal Kr Das Mandal, et al. (2007). In ESNOLA approach, the synthesized output is generated by concatenating the basic signal segments from the signal dictionary at epoch positions. The epochs are most important for signal units, which represent vocalic or quasi-periodic sounds. An epoch position is represented in Figure 2.

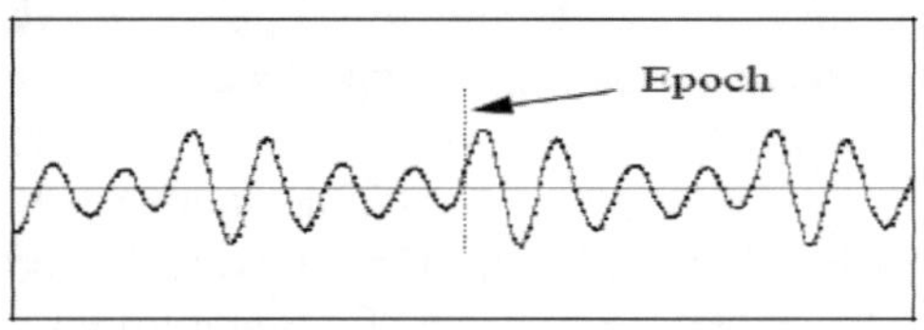

Figure 2: Epoch position of a speech segment

Steady states in the nucleus vowel segment of the synthesized signal are generated by the linear interpolation with appropriate weights of the last period and the first period respectively of the preceding and the succeeding segments. The generated signals require some smoothing at the point of concatenation. This is achieved by a proper windowing of the output signal without hampering the spectral quality.

The synthesized voiced output for the name "ভারত" is shown in Figure 3.

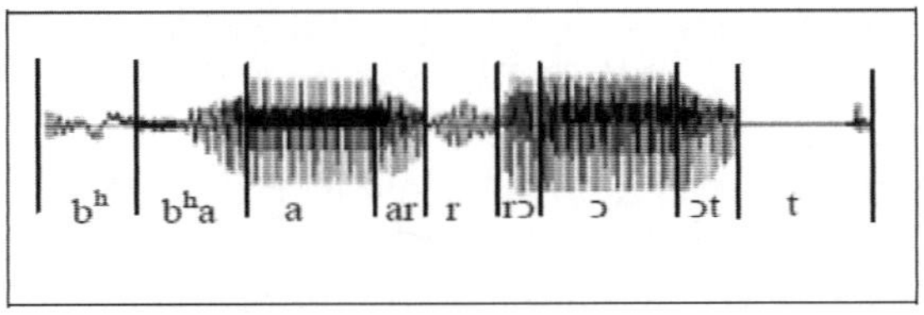

Figure 3: Represent a synthesized voiced output for a given text input / b^{h}arot /

4 Implementation on Android

The exact system specification is shown on Table 1. An Android application will run on a mobile device with limited computing power and storage, and constrained battery life. Because of this, it should be efficient. Following actions are taken to run the application on Android –

Table 1: System Specifications

Features	LG Optimus One P500
Operating System	Android OS, v2.2
Processor	ARM 11
CPU speed	600 MHz
RAM	512 MB
Display	256K colors, TFT
Input method	Touch-screen
Connectivity	USB

4.1 Memory Management

On Android, a Context is an abstract class which is used for many operations but mostly to load and access resources. But keeping a long-lived reference to a Context and preventing the GC (Garbage Collection) from collecting it causes memory leaks issues. But in here this system has to have long-lived objects that needed a context. So to overcome this Application-Context Class is used. This context will live as long as your application is alive and does not depend on the activities life cycle. It is obtained by calling *Activity.getApplication()*. Apart from that the partneme database is kept in external storage card. Owing to memory constraints, the speech output file is deleted after the speech is produced.

4.2 Optimizing the Source Code

On Android virtual method calls are expensive, much more so than instance field lookups. So common object-oriented programming practices are followed and have getters and setters in the public interface.

All total 596 sound files are stored in the partneme database. Total size of the database is 1.0 Mb and application size is 2.26 Mb.

The TTS system has two major functionality. Firstly, it can read the Bengali massage stored in the phones inbox and secondly, user can generate Bengali speech by typing the Bengali word in English alphabet format.

The input text in English alphabet can be keyed in the provided text box (Figure 3). The 'Speak to me' button generates the speech file corresponding to the text keyed in and plays the audio file generated. Graphical user interface is shown in Figure. 4-5.

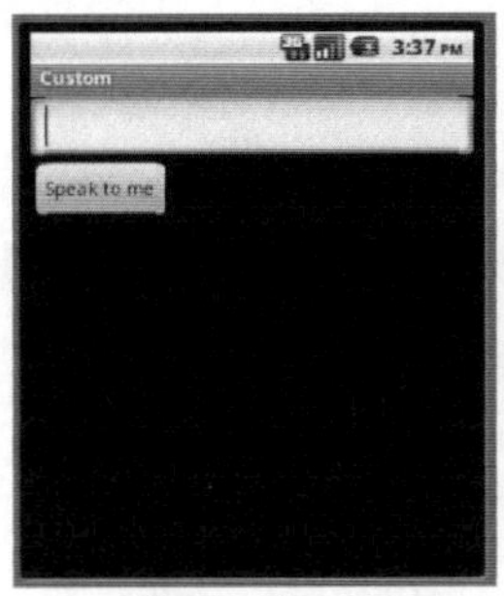

Figure 4

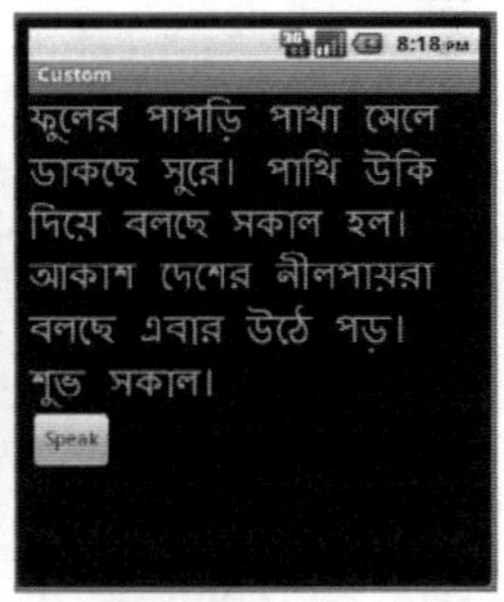

Figure 5

Fig. 4-5 is the internal interface of the application

Application can be distributed to end user directly by developer website or by Android Market an on device application store. This TTS application has not published yet but it can be downloaded on the android device connected to a desktop PC through the USB port.

5 Performance And Quality Evaluation

5.1 Processing Speed Test

Measurement of processing speed is done by counting the synthesis time manually. We started measuring the time when a "speak" button (Figure 5) is pressed until the first speech sound is pronounced. Results are shown in Table 2.

Table 2 speed time test

Utterance (words)	No. of syllables	Processing Speed [in sec.]
2	6	0.45
3	8	0.56
4	11	0.86
5	15	1.19

5.2 Speech Quality Evaluation

To measure the output speech quality 5 subjects, 3 male (L1, L2, L3) and 2 female (L4, L5), are selected and their age ranging from 24 to 50. All subjects are native speakers of Standard Colloquial Bangla and non speech expert. 10 original (as uttered by speaker) and modified (as uttered with android version) sentences are randomly presented for listening and their judgment in 5 point score (1=less natural – 5=most natural). Table 3 represents the tabulated mean opinion scores for all sentences of each subject for original as well as modified sentences.

Table 3 result of listing test

		L1	L2	L3	L4	L5
Modified	Avg	3.82	1.76	2.62	2.73	3.5
Sentences	Stdev	0.73	1.15	0.82	0.81	0.5
Original	Avg	4.91	4.33	4.82	4.76	4.8
Sentences	Stdev	0.11	0.23	0.83	0.42	0.3

The total average score for the original sentences is 4.72 and the modified sentence is 2.88. Figure 6 graphically represents the mean opinion score to visualize the closeness of the employed prosodic rules to the original sentences.

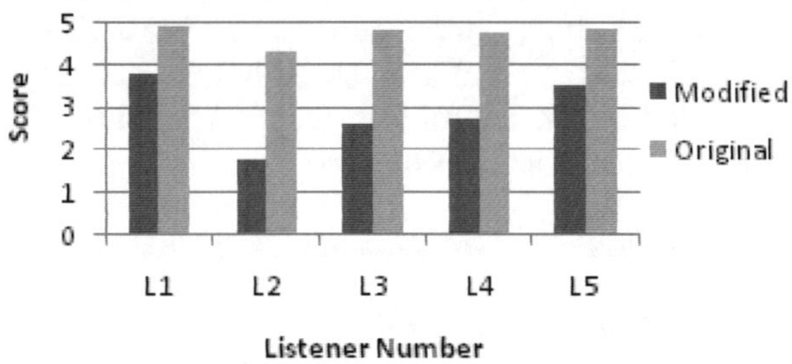

Figure 6: Bar chart of the listening test

6 Conclusion And Future Works

In this paper, we describe our implementation of a Bengali speech synthesizer on a mobile device. Our goal is to develop a text-to-speech (TTS) application that can produce an output speech in almost real-time on an average smart phone. Our synthesizer is based on Epoch Synchronous Non Overlap Add (ESNOLA) suitable for implementing a fast and small TTS application. We modified several components in ESNOLA to make it run on android device. As for the output sound quality of TTS, there is plenty of room for improvement. We also plan to develop a more complete text analysis module which can handle the prosody at the sentence better way.

References

Basu, J., Basu, T., Mitra, M., Mandal, S. 2009. Grapheme to Phoneme (G2P) conversion for Bangla. Speech Database and Assessments, Oriental COCOSDA International Conference, pp. 66-71.

Chatterji Suniti Kumar. 2002. The Original and Development of the Bengali Language. Published by Rupa.Co, ISBN 81-7167-117-9, 1926.

Das Mandal Shyamal Kr, Saha Arup, Sarkar Indranil Datta Asoke Kumar. 2005. Phonological, International & Prosodic Aspects of Concatenative Speech Synthesizer Development for Bangla. Proceeding of SIMPLE-05, pp56-60.

Hoffmann, R et aL. 2003. A Multilingual TTS System with less than 1: MByte Footprint for Embedded Applications. Proceeding of ICASSP.

M. Pucher, and P. Frohlich. 2005. A User Study on the Influence of Mobile Device Class, Synthesis Method, Data Rate and Lexicon on Speech Synthesis Quality. Inter Speech.

P. Tsiakoulis, A. Chalamandaris, S. Karabetsos, and S. Raptis. 2008. A Statistical Method for Database Reduction for Embedded Unit Selection Speech Synthesis. ICASSP, Las Vegas, Nevada, USA.

Sarkar Pabitra. 1990. Bangla Balo. Prama prakasani.

Shyamal Kumar Das Mandal and Asoke Kumar Datta,. 2007. Epoch synchronous non-overlap-add (ESNOLA) method-based concatenative speech synthesis system for Bangla. 6th ISCA Workshop on Speech Synthesis, Germany, pp. 351-355.

W. Black and K. A. Lenzo. 2001. Flite: a small fast nm-time synthesis engine. 4th ISCA Workshop on Speech Synthesis.

Author Index

Association for Computational Linguistics
209 N. Eighth Street
Stroudsburg, Pennsylvania 18360

CURRAN ASSOCIATES INC
proceedings
.com